Cambridge Elements

Elements in Women Theatre Makers
edited by
Elaine Aston
Lancaster University
Melissa Sihra
Trinity College Dublin

ELLEN TERRY, SHAKESPEARE, AND SUFFRAGE IN AUSTRALIA AND NEW ZEALAND

Kate Flaherty
Australian National University

CAMBRIDGE
UNIVERSITY PRESS

Shaftesbury Road, Cambridge CB2 8EA, United Kingdom

One Liberty Plaza, 20th Floor, New York, NY 10006, USA

477 Williamstown Road, Port Melbourne, VIC 3207, Australia

314–321, 3rd Floor, Plot 3, Splendor Forum, Jasola District Centre,
New Delhi – 110025, India

103 Penang Road, #05–06/07, Visioncrest Commercial, Singapore 238467

Cambridge University Press is part of Cambridge University Press & Assessment,
a department of the University of Cambridge.

We share the University's mission to contribute to society through the pursuit of
education, learning and research at the highest international levels of excellence.

www.cambridge.org
Information on this title: www.cambridge.org/9781009559294

DOI: 10.1017/9781009559287

First published 2025

A catalogue record for this publication is available from the British Library

ISBN 978-1-009-55929-4 Hardback
ISBN 978-1-009-55933-1 Paperback
ISSN 2634-2391 (online)
ISSN 2634-2383 (print)

Ellen Terry, Shakespeare, and Suffrage in Australia and New Zealand

Elements in Women Theatre Makers

DOI: 10.1017/9781009559287
First published online: March 2025

Kate Flaherty
Australian National University

Author for correspondence: Kate Flaherty, kate.flaherty@anu.edu.au

Abstract: While the life and career of Ellen Terry (1847–1928) have attracted decades of attention from theatre historians and feminist biographers, one chapter remains hidden: Terry's tour of her solo Shakespeare lectures to Australia and New Zealand in 1914. This bold venture, made at the age of sixty-six, has been interpreted as an indication of Terry's declining physical and mental health following her 1906 Jubilee. Yet Terry claimed that 'while in Australia, although a woman, I am permitted to be a person', testifying affinity with the geopolitical region in which women had already achieved the right to vote in federal elections and to run for parliament. This Element undertakes the first comprehensive examination of the 1914 tour to reveal Terry's professional agency, her creative autonomy, her skilful navigation of ageist sexism, her eager receptivity to new natural environments, and her friendship with international opera star, Nellie Melba.

This Element also has a video abstract: Cambridge.org/EWTM_Flaherty_abstract

Keywords: Ellen Terry, Shakespeare, Australia, New Zealand, Nellie Melba

ISBNs: 9781009559294 (HB), 9781009559331 (PB), 9781009559287 (OC)
ISSNs: 2634-2391 (online), 2634-2383 (print)

Contents

Introduction

While the life and career of Ellen Terry (1847–1928) has attracted decades of attention from theatre historians and feminist biographers, one chapter remains hidden: Terry's tour of her solo Shakespeare lectures to no fewer than twelve cities across Australia and New Zealand in 1914. Until now, this bold venture, made at the age of sixty-six, has been interpreted as an indication of declining physical and mental health, and dismissed as belonging to the 'disoriented, wandering years' that followed her Jubilee.[1] The year 1906 has been established as the apotheosis of Terry's stage career; it was the year of her Jubilee event at Drury Lane and the year in which she played Hermione, the mysterious living statue in Shakespeare's *The Winter's Tale*, at Her Majesty's. What Gail Marshall has called the 'Galatea aesthetic', governed both occasions: 'For Hermione, and for the Victorians', explains Gail Marshall, 'sculpture is a way of achieving [. . .] the association of timeless ideals with women'.[2] Terry scholars have analysed how commemorative and celebratory approaches to Terry's life, such as her Jubilee, perpetuated her youthful identity as 'the painter's actress', by conspiring to fix her meaning. These static figurations were understood, or misunderstood, as reinforcing dominant notions of the nineteenth century's ideal womanhood: passivity, stoicism, and beauty. In the shifting sensibilities of the twentieth century, alternate aspects of her life were thrown into relief. Her public profile as a financially independent working woman saw her singled out as the exemplar of the 'Freewoman' vaunted by the periodical of that title in 1911; and she was made a figurehead for the women's suffrage movement through involvement with her daughter, Edith Craig's political theatre.[3] This makes Auerbach's words apt: 'she mirrored the passing needs of successive phases of culture.'[4]

However, Terry did not 'mirror' passing needs in a passive manner; she participated in the agile and opportunistic formation of her own public profile well beyond her Jubilee. Some of Terry's modes of liberation from entrenchment in the London actor manager system have been ably articulated. Gail Marshall demonstrates how Terry was freed through her writing of personal correspondence, her autobiography, and her lectures.[5] Katharine Cockin examines Terry's collaboration in this process with her daughter, and Craig's partner, Christopher St John, in forging a textual legacy.[6] Lisa Kazmier liberates Terry

---

[1] Auerbach, *Ellen Terry*, p. 8.　　[2] Marshall, *Actresses on the Victorian Stage*, p. 56.

[3] The *Freewoman* I.1 (23 November 1911) quoted in Cockin, *Women and Theatre in the Age of Suffrage*, p. 49.

[4] Auerbach, *Ellen Terry*, p. 17.　　[5] Marshall, *Actresses on the Victorian Stage*.

[6] Cockin, 'Ellen Terry, the Ghost-Writer and the Laughing Statue' and 'Slinging the Ink About'.

retrospectively by highlighting how, through commemoration, Terry's life was distorted by nostalgia to serve nationalist agendas.[7]

These revisionist arguments add historiographical probity to studies of Terry's life and its political significance, winning her an effective, ideological liberation. However, one chapter of Terry's adventurous lived experience remains beyond the purview of these studies – the ambitious tour of her Shakespeare lecture programme to Australia and New Zealand in 1914. None of Terry's family members accompanied her, so the venture hovers at the periphery of their careful custodianship of her image and has consequently fallen out of sight for most, if not all, subsequent biographers and theatre historians.

Nina Auerbach, whose biography has rightly been regarded as authoritative for over three decades, imagines the years of Terry's life following her Jubilee as a period of sad disintegration. She laments that 'the loving response [Terry] received at Drury Lane did not protect her from the twenty-two wandering, disoriented years that lay ahead'.[8] Other scholars taking cues from Auerbach elide or skip over this period. But portraying Terry as a representative British woman making an ill-advised trip 'out' to Australia in old age has occluded understanding of her politically resonant operation as a touring actress. Australia and New Zealand afforded Terry new geographical, discursive, socio-political, and affective relational spaces, and she used these to reconfigure, performatively, her relationship with her own past in ways that are not accounted for in existing biographical and scholarly narratives.

Terry's refusal to be fixed in space and time, her insistence on moving, posed as much of an emotional challenge to her loved ones as it has a methodological one to her latter-day scholars and biographers. The raison d'être for the present volume is that material traces of Terry's Australia and New Zealand tour, many of them only coming to light with digitisation of newspapers and other archival materials, offer a contrast to any account provided to date. For example, in Sydney, Terry sat for a portrait by photographer Rudolph Buchner (see Figure 1). The gleam of light Buchner caught in her intelligent eye is one of many traces of her lively presence in Australia that my Element aims to make visible. Read alongside Terry's letters, interviews and other media reportage convey her wonder, vivacity, and resourcefulness despite ill health and anxiety prompted by the onset of war. Her programme of Shakespeare lectures is revealed as exploiting the freedom of distance from London to critique the actor manager system and to reassert her independent creative agency through performance. Her lectures, letters, and comments to the Australian and New Zealand presses reflect her formulation of a compelling long view of the

---

[7] Kazmier, 'Her Final Performance'.   [8] Auerbach, *Ellen Terry*, p. 5.

Figure 1 'Ellen Terry, English actor', 1914, Rudolph Buchner (photographer), State Library of NSW: Sydney, Australia, P1/1739; https://collection.sl.nsw .gov.au/record/93QVrDN1 (Out of copyright: created before 1955)

struggle for women's suffrage. Her friendship with international opera star, Nellie Melba, is unveiled as a sustaining bond that transforms foreign soil into a relational space of solidarity.

Un-retiring Actress

The year 1906, in which Terry celebrated her Jubilee, was not a year for slowing down. Having toured to America seven times during her Lyceum years with Henry Irving, she packed her bags in her sixtieth year and made the familiar voyage in 1907. In 1910 she did so again, this time with a new programme of lectures on Shakespeare. In 1914, still not satisfied to stand still at the age of sixty-six, and against her doctor's advice, she agreed to a proposal by the actor manager Joseph Blascheck to take her lectures on an extensive tour of Australia and New Zealand.[9] She opened in Melbourne on the 7th of May and did not return to London until May of the following year.[10]

Terry sailed on the *SS Omrah* from London to Melbourne via Naples, Port Said, Suez and Colombo (see Figure 2). She landed in Fremantle in Western Australia before continuing by sea around the southern coast of Australia to Melbourne. There she gave three performances at the Town Hall on the 7th, 9th, and 11th of May. She continued north to Sydney by rail where she gave three more lectures at the Town Hall on the 14th, 16th, and 18th of May, and then travelled north again by rail to Brisbane for two more lectures on 21st and 23rd May, before returning to Sydney on 24th May.

Figure 2 'Orient Steam Navigation Company liner *Omrah* in Brisbane in 1914', (no date); photographic print: black & white, State Library of Queensland; https://collections.slq.qld.gov.au/viewer/IE1399323
(public domain; copyright expired)

---

[9] Manvell says that she was 'warned against the tour on the grounds that her heart was showing strain'. See Manvell, *Ellen Terry*, p. 314.

[10] Ibid, p. 315.

The staggering scale of distances Terry traversed during these first few weeks in Australia has received little attention. In seventeen days, the sixty-six-year-old actress gave eight performances in three cities and covered almost 3,000 kilometres overland (comparable to the distance from London to Moscow). On the 26th of May, back in Sydney, she addressed a letter to her daughter in which she makes the hardly surprising claim: 'The journeys by ship & train have nearly killed me = Tomorrow we go over to New Zealand & I take 8 or 10 days rest.'[11] This is not an expression of geriatric fragility; even today her punishing schedule would take its toll on the youngest and fittest of performers.

A difficult three-day crossing of the Tasman to Auckland landed Terry in New Zealand on the 31st May.[12] She rested at the popular thermal resort of Rotorua for just over a week.[13] She then opened in Auckland on the 11th of June and resumed her energetic pace of touring: Auckland, Wanganui, Wellington, Napier. Crossing to the South Island, she performed in Dunedin, Timaru, and Christchurch, returning to the North Island for another performance in Wellington before re-crossing the Tasman to Sydney.

On the 28th of July, Terry was hosted at a benefit event by the Actors' Association in Sydney, shortly after which she evidently rested again in Jenner private hospital[14] in Potts Point overlooking Sydney Harbour. She then returned to the upmarket Oriental Hotel – her regular abode in Melbourne (see Figure 3). At the onset of war in August, her passage home seemed uncertain, and entertainment business had dried up. She turned her energy to the war effort, performing in at least five charitable fund-raising concerts: two matinees in Melbourne on the 28th of August; and, with Nellie Melba, a grand concert at the Melbourne Auditorium on the 10th of September followed by two smaller concerts – at Lilydale on the 14th of September and at Warburton on the 16th of September.[15] Throughout September and October, she was hosted frequently, along with other actors, at Melba's rural home in the Yarra Valley, outside of Melbourne.

On the 29th of October, Terry boarded the *Makura* in Sydney for Vancouver via Auckland;[16] on the 23rd of November she boarded a train for New York.[17] From there she made forays to present her re-named 'Scenes from Shakespeare' to audiences in Boston, Detroit, and Los Angeles.[18] In late February of 1915 she

---

[11] Terry and Cockin, *The Collected Letters* V6. (1741. 'To Edith Craig, 26 May [1914]'), p. 14.

[12] 'Ellen Terry: Arrival in Auckland', *Auckland Star* (NZ) 1 June 1914, p. 7.

[13] Untitled, *Poverty Bay Herald Poverty Bay Herald*, 10 June 1914, p. 2.

[14] Terry and Cockin, *The Collected Letters* V6. (1748. 'To Edith Craig, 30 July [1914]'), p. 22.

[15] 'Madame Melba's Aid', *The Australasian*, 19 September 1914, p. 28.

[16] 'Dramatic Notes', *Leader*, 24 October 1914, p. 37.

[17] Terry and Cockin, *The Collected Letters* V6. (1760. 'To Edith Craig, 26 May [1914]'), p. 39.

[18] 'Amusements: Ellen Terry', *The Star-independent* (Harrisburg), 21 January 1914.

                    Women Theatre Makers

Figure 3 'Oriental Hotel', Collins Street, Melbourne, Vic. Lindt, J. W. (John William) 1845–1926, photographer; State Library of Victoria: Melbourne, Australia; https://viewer.slv.vic.gov.au/?entity=IE1549108&mode=browse (out of copyright).

had surgery at the New York Eye and Ear Infirmary to restore her failing eyesight.[19] On the 1st of May she boarded the *SS New York* in New York, and sailed for Liverpool, finally arriving in London to be reunited with her family and friends.[20]

This expedition, if made by a younger woman, would be understood as bold and enterprising. However, Auerbach's otherwise intricately detailed account of Terry's life describes it in this way:

> [S]he went off to Australia alone with Shakespeare when she was 66. Before war was declared in August she broke down.[21]

In this dismissal of Terry's 1914 tour as an embarrassing, ill-judged episode of overreaching culminating in accelerated decline, Auerbach and Manvell take cues from someone much closer to Terry. Christopher St John was the long-term

---

[19] Terry and Cockin, *The Collected Letters* V6. (1779. 'To Edith Craig, 16 February 1915'), p. 70.
[20] 'Ellen Terry Sails for Home', *New York Tribune*, 2 May 1915, p. 3.
[21] Auerbach, *Ellen Terry*, p. 442.

partner of Terry's daughter, Edith Craig.[22] In her expanded introduction to the 1933 edition of Terry's autobiography – *Ellen Terry's Memoirs* – St John describes the 1914 tour as 'exertion and excitement and eventual disappointment'.[23]

Christopher St John, to whom we owe much for the publication of Terry's autobiography and lectures, was the first manager of her official character arc. An anxiety about Terry's reputation that clearly exceeded her own animates these narratives of 'eventual disappointment', and 'disorientated wandering', implying a desire to preserve Terry in both time and space as a respectable, representative figure. The effect is of a benevolent stage manager closing the curtain on a performer who is not ready to leave the stage. Without question, Terry's experience in Australia and New Zealand was mixed: chequered with serious bouts of illness, fraught with failure, disappointment, and anxiety. Terry's own correspondence and media coverage of her tour make this plain. But if we peel back the unconscious double bias of an ageist and imperialistic world view, these factors should make her adventure all the more intriguing.

Christopher St John's version of Terry's tour to Australia and New Zealand, taken up by latter-day biographers and scholars, is a story of Terry wilfully abandoning her own story. It relegates geographical zones as beyond narrowly national, biographical interest even though they were well within the ambit of Terry's curiosity. This Element makes Terry a case study for how national celebrity can obscure the wider creative personal and political legacies of women theatre makers. The more closely I read Terry's letters and examine the media reporting on her tour, the more I find that is at odds with the widely accepted dismissal of the venture. I construct an alternative character arc for Terry which revels in the complexity of her antipodean adventure. It is no less a character arc than the old one, but it is grounded in new evidence. It is also impelled by revisionary developments in theatre history and insights from the spatial turn that demand new critical attention to discourses of age and space.

By undertaking the first comprehensive study of Terry's tour to Australia and New Zealand, this Element takes a phenomenological slant; it offers a differently situated narrative that prioritises Terry's point of view in dialogue with local perspectives rather than the views of those she left behind. Terry claimed that 'while in Australia, although a woman, I am permitted to be a person', testifying affinity with the geopolitical region in which women had already achieved the right to vote in federal elections and to run for

---

[22] On converting to Catholicism, 'Christabel Marshall' had taken on the name Christopher St. John; in this Element, in keeping with St John's personal correspondence and all succeeding scholarship, female pronouns are retained.

[23] Terry, Craig, and John, *Ellen Terry's Memoirs*, p. 289.

parliament.[24] This is an astonishing statement for its existential and affective intensity. Whether Terry spoke it to please her new public or whether it expressed a deeply felt liberation is difficult to say. In either case it raises new questions about the impact of transnational mobility on the self-understanding and convictions of the artist. The Element will use insights from the spatial turn to explore how transnational mobility made Terry a vector of political change in ways for which existing transatlantic life narratives have failed to account.

Feminist Approaches to Space and Touring

The spatial turn in cultural studies culminates in a realisation that the meaning of space and spaces is not given but produced through discourses and social practices. This entails a critique of the imperialist paradigm that sees the world as comprising political and cultural centres and margins. 'Globalectics' supplies an apt counter-concept for my purposes; Ngũgĩ wa Thiong'o points out that the surface of a sphere has no centre; every place is a centre for someone; every 'there' a 'here', and every 'then' a 'now'. This approach embraces 'wholeness, interconnectedness, equality of potentiality of parts'.[25]

For theatre studies the spatial turn has led to new curiosity about touring theatre – the 'here' and 'now' of touring theatre being necessarily distant from the traditional, nationally determined, 'centres' of culture. Christopher Balme's 2019 study of actor-manager and agent Daniel E. Bandmann's touring enterprises might be seen as establishing a 'first phase of globalisation ... from the opening of the Suez Canal in 1869 to the outbreak of World War I in 1914'.[26] Building upon Balme's interest in global networks is the series 'Transnational Theatre Histories' (Palgrave), which includes Nic Leonhardt's 2021 title: *Theatres across Oceans: Mediators of Transatlantic Exchange (1890–1925)*. Leonhardt concentrates on male and female theatrical agents – behind-the-scenes enablers of transnational theatre – and their exploitation of the emerging global networks of transport, communication and media. In her first chapter, she demonstrates how the nodal structure of networks that characterised theatre in this era resulted in an expanded global imagination. In this Element, the eclectic programmes of the patriotic concerts in which Ellen Terry took part in Victoria in 1914 offer a clear example of this evolving global imagination.

Other related work on space has provided an important stimulus for this volume by foregrounding 'feminist' geographies. Philosopher Gillian Rose, geographer Doreen Massey, and other cultural geographers have uncovered how discourses of space and spatialised divisions of labour have been

---

[24] 'Arrival of Miss Ellen Terry', *The Queenslander*, Saturday 30 May 1914, p. 6.
[25] Thiong'o, *Globaletics,* p. 8, 60.   [26] Balme, *The Globalization of Theatre*, p. 4.

implicated in complex ways in class and gender inequality.[27] Feminist historians have established fruitful intersections with these developments. One influential example for my study of Terry is Deacon, Russell, and Woollacott's volume *Transnational Lives: Biographies of Global Modernity, 1700-present*. This work resists imperialist paradigms in which nation defines experience, exploring, instead, 'the potential of individual life stories to explicate worlds', including the possibilities of 'self-transformation entailed in mobility and modernity'.[28] Another relevant example is Beebe and Davis's *Space, Place and Gendered Identities: Feminist History and the Spatial Turn*, which offers temporally and culturally diverse case studies of how place and space shape gendered meaning and experience.[29]

Here and elsewhere, my particular focus is on the striking figure cut by the touring actress of the fin de siècle period. She occupies and transforms the meaning of public space, traverses transnational space, and contrives domestic space in many places in a period when her rights, including her right to vote, to own property, and to have custody of her children, are being fiercely contested. Consequently, my co-edited volume *Touring Performance and Global Exchange (1850–1960): Making Tracks* has an unabashed focus on the experiences of touring women theatre makers. Working with Gilli-Bush Bailey 'across the oceans' on that collection also revealed to me how professional friendship can redefine space and distance. This in turn sparked my interest in the friendship between Ellen Terry and Nellie Melba.

'Space is now no longer seen as a physical territorial concept but as a relational one', asserts Doris Bachmann-Medick of the change ushered in by the spatial turn, foregrounding dynamic connections and the complex networks over categories of nation or region. 'A central element in the spatial turn is not territorial space as a container or a vessel, but space as a social production process encompassing perceptions, utilizations and appropriations.'[30] This is the definition of space I invoke to guide the present study – I seek to tease out how Terry's 'perceptions, utilizations and appropriations' of geographic, discursive, sociopolitical, and affective spaces can spur a revaluation of the intrepid step she took by touring her Shakespeare lectures to Australia and New Zealand in 1914.

Summary of Sections

Section 1 revisits the question of why, at the age of sixty-six, and with known medical conditions, Terry made the decision to tour Australia and New Zealand.

---

[27] Rose, *Feminism and Geography*; Massey, *Space, Place, and Gender*.

[28] Deacon, Russell, and Woollacott, 'Introduction', pp. 5, 7.

[29] Beebe and Davis, (eds.) *Space, Place and Gendered Identities*.

[30] Bachmann-Medick, *Cultural Turns*, p. 216.

The standard narrative, following Christopher St John's lead, has explained the decision solely in terms of Terry's age-addled belligerence about providing for her family. I expand on this account by exploring the evidence for equally plausible and more positive drivers. The disappointment ascribed to the tour by St John and later commentators was a foregone conclusion: Terry was warned about 'not living up to' the reputation she had established and thereby risked her prestige by making the tour. These threats were contradicted by swathes of positive reception but, unsurprisingly, realised by some vicious, pointedly ageist, and misogynist attacks in the press. I query the warnings and the attacks, showing that they both belong to a prejudicially gendered discourse of ageing. I provide evidence for how Terry met the warnings and threats head-on with good humour and creative intelligence. I also show how, like other actresses before her, she performed her ageing to her own advantage in ways that spoke to socio-political exigencies in the contexts in which she performed. Countering all prior accounts of the 1914 tour, I suggest that her age and the geographical expanse she chose to traverse constituted spaces of opportunity. If these opportunities were partly unforeseen by Terry in her setting out, her exploitation of them is all the more remarkable and worthy of scholarly attention.

Section 2 extends this consideration of physical and temporal spaces into the discursive space of Terry's 'Shakespeare discourses'. I challenge the traditional view of this repertoire as a weak echo of Terry's real stage career and at best an opportunity to 'relive' her greatest moments on the stage.[31] As others have recognised, the Shakespeare discourses were a revisionary intervention into and critique of the London actor manager system. They created a discursive space in which Terry could evolve and exercise authoritative acts of interpretation and political persuasion. I also aim to nuance the more recent classification of the discourses as belonging to Terry's written legacy with the static fixity this implies. Instead, I reveal them as 'moving devices', virtuosic, demanding, and performatively agile in their response to the contexts to which touring exposed them.

One of the key contextual contrasts between Terry's home and her tour destinations in 1914 was their uneven progress in the international movement for women's suffrage. Women in New Zealand had exercised a right to vote for twenty years; women in Australia had been eligible to vote and to run for seats in federal parliament for twelve years. For women in England, these prerogatives would be many years in coming. Through involvement with her daughter, Edith Craig's activist troupe called The Pioneer Players, Terry was already part of a front of creative public agitation aiming to bring about women's suffrage. Section 3 begins by outlining her participation in these political dramas. It then

---

[31] Manvell, *Ellen Terry*, p. 313.

maps the relations between New Zealand, Australia, and Britain with respect to the contrasting phases and cultures of their campaigns for women's suffrage to illuminate the extent to which Terry's tour constituted movement between contrasting but connected geopolitical spaces. By drawing evidence from Terry's correspondence with Edith during the tour, and from newspaper interviews in Australia, New Zealand, and the United States, the section will show how Terry's convictions and reflections on the movement were shaped by the geopolitical environments through which she moved. Further, it will reveal how the political import of the Shakespeare discourses was inflected by the places and the people with whom she interacted.

Section 4 returns the focus to more literal spaces. It examines Terry's affective relationships with the natural environment and with Nellie Melba in their time shared – both on the public stage and at Melba's rural property. Evidence suggests that Terry's health improved markedly throughout September and October across three visits with Melba. Although homesick, Terry seems to have experienced Melba's domestic hospitality, philanthropic and creative energy and circle of acquaintance as a kind of home connected imaginatively with her own. Importantly, the relationship between Terry and Melba offers an avenue for exploring both their prominence and precarity as international women theatre makers in the first era of global conflict. It reveals the threats they weathered and the function of the sociable and professional networks they established through their transnational mobility. Bringing such networks into focus challenges the narratives that define the interest and importance of touring experience by youth and in inverse proportion to miles travelled from the centre of Anglophone culture or 'home'. In Terry and Melba's friendship we can see a world made newly navigable by imaginative and relational sympathies.

1 'Not all there': Age and Distance

On account of her age and fragile health, Ellen Terry's family and friends tried to dissuade her from making a tour of her Shakespeare lectures to Australia and New Zealand before the outbreak of war in 1914. Notwithstanding, she made the tour and went on to live for a further fourteen years. While most newspaper commentators in Australia and New Zealand were warm in her praise, others condemned her for imposing herself on new audiences at such a late stage in her career. This section will demonstrate how theatre history and biographical scholarship have failed to challenge the ageist and gendered discrimination implicit in these assessments. It will show how the imperative to fix Terry as the ideal British woman within the 'sculptural aesthetic' that dominated her 1906 Jubilee has in some ways gone on to influence even feminist revisionist accounts of her life.[32] To do so the section marshals new evidence of how Terry performatively negotiated the discourse of aging and points to some of the implications of this spatially literate approach to time and distance that unfolds in later sections.

1.1 Perils of Travel

Both biographers Nina Auerbach and Roger Manvell see Terry's choice to make a tour of her Shakespeare lectures to Australia and New Zealand in 1914 as indicative of, and contributing to, her decline. Auerbach moves back and forth between 1912 and 1928 in the final chapter of her biography entitled 'Child', figuring Australia and New Zealand as a zone of despondent and irrevocable self-exile from adult independence.

This narrative inflection is attributable to Christopher St John. St John collaborated intensively with Terry in the later years of her life in the publication of her memoirs – *The Story of My Life* (1908) – and in the development of her Shakespeare lectures. St John also provided an introduction to the lectures, first published four years after Terry's death in 1932. As scholars have recognised, St John's influence within Terry's legacy is complicated.[33] It is because of St John that so much of Terry's life-writing is published. St John's analytical framing has supplied a political coherence to Terry's life story and, as discussed in Section 3, St John's and Edith Craig's activism for women's suffrage provided channels for politicisation of Terry's creative output in her post-Jubilee career. However, with respect to Terry's 1914–15 venture, St John's shaping influence is more conservative that we might expect.

In the posthumous 1933 edition of Terry's autobiography (re-published by Craig and St John as *Ellen Terry's Memoirs*, 'with preface, notes and additional biographical chapters'), St John uses interpretative para-text to wield strong control over what was first published in 1908 as Terry's *My Story*. She frames Terry's motivation for going to Australia as misguided if gallant self-sacrifice. St John reports that Terry was advised by her lawyer that she could retire and avoid the trip if she reduced her payments to her children and grandchildren and relinquished her plan to provide them with an income after her death. That same day, states St John, Terry confirmed her plans to travel to Australia.[34] In this memorialising project, Terry's pleasure and creative ambition play little part. Faithfully transcribing selections from Terry's correspondence, St John

---

[32] For the 'sculptural' or 'Galatea' aesthetic, see Gail Marshall's analysis in *Actresses on the Victorian Stage*, p. 56.

[33] See Cockin's discussion of St John's potentially 'distorting' influence on Terry's memoirs in 'Ellen Terry, the Ghost-Writer and the Laughing Statue', p. 158.

[34] Terry, Craig, and John, *Ellen Terry's Memoirs*, p. 289.

sums up that the tour was 'exertion and excitement and eventual disappointment', which Terry 'survived' despite her failing health.[35]

In the wake of St John's account, anxiety over finances has served as
a comprehensive explanation for Terry's seemingly radical step of touring
Australia and New Zealand. Roger Manvell explains that as financial pressures
from Terry's dependents mounted, her success in winning major roles diminished. He describes her as a 'respected public figure appearing in parts of ever
decreasing importance until she was reduced, in advanced years, to one-night
stands in the provinces'.[36] In her introduction to Volume 6 of Terry's letters,
Katharine Cockin records Terry's rationalisation of her property holdings in
response to financial pressure just before departure for Australia, and points out
that Australia and New Zealand, unlike America, offered new markets. With the
observation that Terry was 'naturally open to new experiences and places',
however, Cockin acknowledges that the prospect of the tour was, perhaps, not
purely a grim necessity to Terry.[37]

Terry's family and friends exerted emotional pressure on Terry to give up the
tour. Manvell records that her doctor advised against the trip on grounds of
health. St John quotes Terry's business manager asking, 'Why risk your prestige
in a strange land at your time of life?' He warned her that 'Australians who had
never seen her act would be attracted to her lectures only by her reputation, and
might think that in them she hardly lived up to it'.[38] This reflects an assumption
that Terry's best work was behind her and that her lectures were a diminished
version of her real (former) self.

Despite all this, Terry could not be dissuaded from her tour. Evidence
suggests there was a range of impelling and compelling factors that fortified
her resolution, but biographical and critical scholarship has made little effort to
come to terms with them. In terms of push factors, for example, it is broadly
acknowledged that Terry's relationship with her adult daughter Edith was, while
loving, fraught. Manvell claims that Edith's possessiveness had a role in Terry's
judicial separation from her husband James Carew.[39] Auerbach takes a more
compassionate view of the entanglement, suggesting that from the 1890s
onwards, Edith (or Edy as she was known) had begun to 'mother' and to
'manage' her own mother, to whom she was, conversely, indispensable.[40]
Even so, there has been no suggestion that this predicament may have enhanced
the appeal of a several months' separation for both women. As we have seen,

---

[35] Ibid. p. 289.   [36] Manvell, *Ellen Terry*, p. 313.
[37] Cockin, 'Introduction', in Terry and Cockin, *The Collected Letters* V6. 1745. 'To Edith Craig,
     16–19 June [1914]', p. xiii.
[38] Terry, Craig, and St. John, *Ellen Terry's Memoirs*, p. 289.
[39] Manvell, *Ellen Terry*, p. 303 and p. 310.   [40] Auerbach, *Ellen Terry*, p. 380.

there is plentiful evidence of the financial dependence upon her of Terry's adult offspring during her post-Jubilee career, but little speculation as to the claustrophobic emotional climate from which a trip to Australia and New Zealand might well have represented respite.

However, it is in conceiving of the compelling factors for the tour that twentieth-century scholars most lacked imagination. If money was the motive, then Terry's chosen destinations were rather obvious than Quixotic. As gold rush locations from 1850 onwards, Victoria, New South Wales, and New Zealand were firmly established as lucrative locations on the international touring circuit. Many British and American performers visited, and some made their fortunes. George Selth Coppin, Charles and Ellen Kean, Dion Boucicault, and Daniel E. Bandmann are among the most well-known examples. The international celebrity Charlotte Cushman announced a visit to Australia in 1874 as she neared the age of sixty, but was prevented by illness from fulfilling it.[41] Sarah Bernhardt visited Sydney in 1891, staying at 'The Australian' – the same glamorous hotel in which Terry would stay. Observing the movements of her forerunners and peers, and raised in an itinerant thespian family, it is unlikely that Terry found the prospect of a trip to Australia and New Zealand as daunting as her circle of near acquaintances did. As I point out in Section 2, she described the visit as long deferred and, as explored in Section 4, she expressed detailed, informed curiosity about specific features of Australian and New Zealand flora and landscape. This bespeaks a positive anticipation that has no place in extant explanations for why she made the tour.

Terry was alive to the risks to health and reputation entailed in making such a voyage as a sixty-six-year-old woman, but she responded with canny creative skill to prejudicial attitudes. In an interview in London before her departure, we observe her harnessing the opposition she faced to set up an image of spirited defiance. The interview quoted below was with *The Standard*, but it is worth noting that the New Zealand *Star* reproduces it in a column entitled 'For Women Folk':

> How do I feel about going so far away? Why, as happy as possible for I know that I will return full of renewed life and energy .... Like the captain of the *Pinafore* I am 'never, never sick at sea', and weather, fine or 'dirt' as the sailors call it, invigorates me, and I feel – well a good deal younger than I ought to feel.[42]

The *Star* quotes the *Standard*'s description of Terry's 'long limbs', 'still supple in their movements', and her playful self-derision: '"Lectures! Think of me

<hr>

[41] 'News of the Day', *Evening News* (Sydney: 1869–1931), Friday 27 March 1874, p. 2.

[42] 'For Women Folk', *Star* (Christchurch, NZ), 13 April 1914, p. 7.

lecturing!" And Miss Terry rose to pace the room.' Notice how Terry's physical energy and rejection of formal constraint take centre stage; it is as if she is already speaking to the sensibilities of her antipodean audience.

Although Terry received a warm and respectful welcome in both Australia and New Zealand, as predicted, her age was something to be discursively negotiated. In the vein of *The Standard* above, before her arrival, many commentators remarked on her sprightly girlishness. 'She is now 65 years of age', proclaimed the NZ paper, *Northern Advocate*, (already mistaking her for younger than she was) 'and is still young, her vitality being amazing'.[43] In other instances her ageing appearance was celebrated as augmenting her stately attractiveness and power:

> Miss Terry is very like her portraits, the strong, fine expressive features, softened with the glory of her snow-white hair, surrounding the face with a halo.[44]

In a different key, some reviewers of her lectures saw the virtue of her performances as being in the reflected glory of her past career that they had come to know and love, either through seeing her in London or through the extensive coverage she had received in Australian and New Zealand newspapers.

Although an outlier in terms of its vicious scandal mongering, the popular periodical *Truth* – owned and edited by John Norton – evinces malice towards Terry.[45] It seems to fulfil the predictions about age and reputation that were made in a well-meaning vein by her family and friends. The piece quoted below takes its title from *Hamlet* and is laced with that character's misogyny: 'LOOK HERE UPON THIS PICTURE – AND UPON THIS'. It continues,

> In the gay, giddy and golden girlhood of Ellen Terry she was 'all there', and now that there's more of her she is not all there.
>
> If [...] she is doing the trip for the good of her health, then I say she should be allowed to do it and not become an infliction on the Australian people who have never done her any wrong. Would it not have been better had Ellen Terry been allowed to retire on her laurels? Instead of cavorting on the stage at her present great age, she should be home between the blankets. I do not say she should go, get her to a nunnery; on the contrary I say, in the words of "Lady Macbeth" – TO BED! TO BED!! TO BED!!![46]

---

[43] 'Ellen Terry: Arrival in Australia', *Northern Advocate*, 1 May 1914, p. 5.

[44] 'Arrival of Miss Ellen Terry', *The Queenslander*, 30 May 1914, p. 6.

[45] Cannon, 'Norton, John (1858–1916)', *Australian Dictionary of Biography*, National Centre of Biography, Australian National University, https://adb.anu.edu.au/biography/norton-john-7863/text13663, published first in hardcopy 1988, accessed online 30 August 2024.

[46] 'Lights-O'-Lunnon', Special for *Truth* by Mary Brown; Melbourne 30 May 1914.

Combining a jibe at her changing body with the implication of dementia and a pointed sexual slur, the piece reflects the whole range of cruel gendered derision Terry dared to encounter by coming to Australia.

Terry's adventurousness interpreted as over-reaching was still the theme of commentary in New Zealand in 1927 when news reached the *Northern Advocate* that Terry, now back in England, had broken her arm. With the headline 'Holding on Too Long' the newspaper reports:

> There is particular pathos attaching to the accident which befell Dame Ellen Terry a few days ago, when the one-time great actress fell down a flight of stairs and broke a forearm.

After a brief survey of her career as the 'idol of the British stage', the writer proceeds with moral censure:

> There was a moment when she could have retired in a blaze of glory – when her fame was at its zenith. But love of the profession and devotion to the art which had captivated her, held her to the boards. Old age crept on until . . . [a]t last the final bow was made. It was an exit very different from what it would have been had the psychological moment been seized by the gifted woman.

The writer reveals that the supposedly belated 'final bow' was the tour Terry made to New Zealand in 1914. He opines that 'the tragedy of it hurt those who had seen the wonderful woman enacting as to the life the famous roles of which she was then giving imperfect readings'. The moral of the tale is delivered:

> And now, bowed beneath years, stricken with blindness, and forgotten by the world, Ellen Terry awaits behind the scenes, the end that comes to everybody. It is an incident such as this which gives weight to the Psalmist's words about a time to be born and a time to die.[47]

The reporter, who does not know Ecclesiastes from the Psalms, implies that Terry's fall is the result of a performance tour made thirteen years earlier. This reflects that the ageist reading of Terry's tour as misguided and of-a-piece with her later decline was widespread, even in her lifetime.

In this prejudice we also see the dark side of international celebrity. Private person is conflated with public identity through the metaphor of theatre – she 'awaits behind the scenes, the end'. Terry is conceived as ageing public property in the international imaginary. Her accident provides a pivot point for ruminations upon youth and age on a national scale. 'Even in New Zealand', concludes the journalist, 'in less than a century, there are many notable instances' of people dying at 'the right moment'.[48]

---

[47] 'Holding on Too Long', *Northern Daily Advocate* (New Zealand) Saturday 2 April 1927, p. 4.
[48] Ibid.

1.2 Acting Her Age

The year 1914 was not only a watershed moment for Terry, it was also a distinctive moment of tension in self-definition for Australia and New Zealand. Their participation in the Great War, controversial in both countries, operated as a complex signifier of loyalty to the British Empire and 'birth' as new nations. In light of this, media coverage of Terry's tour reveals that her presence in Australia and New Zealand drew out affinities and anxieties about new nationhood and the aging empire. As Charles and Ellen Kean had discovered as early as 1863 in Melbourne, visitors who traded too much on their imperial credentials were not well received.[49] In the 1914 atmosphere of heightened nationalism and contentious loyalty to empire, Terry had to frame her allegiances carefully.

Terry's first appearances in Australia in the Melbourne Town Hall on the 7th, 8th, and 9th of May produced the kind of ambivalence which could easily have soured into critical scorn and financial failure. 'Miss Ellen Terry was scarcely heard to advantage in Melbourne, although upon each night there was an improvement', remarks an even-handed reviewer for the social magazine *Table Talk*. The inappropriateness of the Town Hall and its acoustic are taken into account but still the reviewer describes Terry as 'out of health' and appearing 'restless', 'anxious', and 'nervy' and among many laudatory observations, claims that 'the fact that 'Miss Terry seems to doubt her memory and reads nearly all her matter, detracts from the effect of her discourses'.[50]

In these first performances, hampered by nerves and a rigidly formal venue, Terry risked disaster by reinforcing the sense of distance her audiences felt from what most of them understood as their cultural origins. As the reviewer makes explicit, Australians wanted 'intimacy' and ease. With remarkable speed, Terry learned to adapt both her performances and her public rhetoric to harmonise with this desire. What Nina Auerbach detects as her early-developed pattern of 'learn[ing] herself by watching others watch her' was demonstrably still in place for the sixty-six-year-old Terry in Australia and New Zealand.[51] The stakes were very high and, attuned to the desires of her public, Terry played an expert hand.

Terry deflected the early notes of disappointment evident in both Australian and New Zealand reception of her Shakespeare lectures by foregrounding her age with self-effacing good humour. As a New Zealand journalist for *Woman's World* interviewing Terry on the 4th of February, prior to her departure from London, recorded:

---

[49] See Flaherty and Lamb, 'The 1863 Melbourne Shakespeare War', p. 17.
[50] 'Miss Ellen Terry', *Table Talk*, 14 May 1914, p. 10.   [51] Auerbach, *Ellen Terry*, p. 17.

> 'Don't let New Zealanders picture me young and dazzlingly beautiful', she
> begged laughingly. 'I am so afraid that they won't realise that it is an old
> woman coming out to see them'.[52]

Repeatedly throughout her tour, Terry joked that 'every woman under thirty believes she is an actress. And every actress believes she is under thirty'.[53] Terry's knowing and defiant sense of humour about her age, her capacity to accept and acknowledge the changes to her appearance while embodying the creative and imaginative continuities with her youth, provide one reason to challenge the relegation of Terry's tour to Australia and New Zealand to a 'seventh age' of disintegration within her life narrative.

Further impetus is added by recent scholarly interest in the ageing actress and critique of gendered discourse around age and female performers.[54] For at least two decades, scholarship has grappled with patterns of invisibility and exclusion of older women, especially in the modern film industry – to which Terry herself was a late life-stage entrant.[55] But compounding these patterns, Kathleen Woodward has suggested that 'ageism is entrenched within feminism itself' – preoccupied as it is with issues associated with the earlier life stages of women.[56] If ageing, like gender and other markers of social difference, is, as Woodward maintains, 'in large part socially constructed', if 'meanings are attached to the figures of age and ageing based on society's evaluation of ageing', then age is linked to performativity and, in Terry's particular case, to performance.[57] Terry performed age and ageing in ways that augmented her own evolving agenda during her visit to Australia and New Zealand and in ways that meshed with sociopolitical exigencies of the contexts in which she performed.

In this she was doing as others before her had done. In 2005, Shearer West identified the ways in which the first female 'superstar' Sarah Siddons manipulated her public image through media and artistic depiction to sustain her prominence and popularity into old age:

> The changes in the physical and iconic bodies of Siddons were negotiated by
> artists, critics and Siddons herself to create an enduring double vision of the
> actress as a queen during a period of nationalistic royalism and political
> instability.[58]

In distinct but comparable ways, I argue that the aged body of Ellen Terry served political purposes in Australia and New Zealand in 1914 that a young actress

---

[52] 'Woman's World: Ellen Terry at Home, an Unconventional Interview, Exuberantly Youthful at Sixty-Six', *Patea Mail* (New Zealand), 27 March 1914, p. 1.

[53] 'Opinion of an Actress', *The Bennington Evening Banner*, 13 January 1915, image 2.

[54] For example, Liddy, *Women, Ageing and the Screen Industries*.

[55] D. Jermyn, 'Get a Life, Ladies'.   [56] See Woodward, *Figuring Age*, pp. ix–xi.

[57] See Woodward, *Figuring Age*, p. x.   [58] West, Siddons, Celebrity and Regality, p. 192.

could not. In Section 3, I will examine how she served, especially in New Zealand, as a heroic veteran from the British front of the battle for women's suffrage; and in Section 4, I will uncover how Terry's participation in war-effort events with Nellie Melba testified reassuringly to the robust bonds of empire as expeditionary forces prepared to leave for the fronts of Europe. Both of these context-specific ways of seeing Terry demonstrate how age signifies differently in different geopolitical spaces.

The geographical distance from London and from family and friends was painful to Terry, but it also facilitated new wonder at the natural world, sated a thirst for adventure, and opened a space for reflection and critique not possible in destinations closer to home. Terry's age also entailed hardships of erratic illness. By the same token, the time that had transpired since the peak of Terry's career success was a space of opportunity for re-configuration which signified authority, tradition, and transnational ties that were of particular significance to Australians and New Zealanders on the brink of war.

For all these reasons it is important to pay more attention to the double vanishing act that Ellen Terry performed by visiting Australian and New Zealand at the age of sixty-six. There is a trove of evidence to suggest that her absence from 'home' in England and from family and friends was not an absence from herself. Against the cruel implication that she was 'not all there', I maintain that her presence in Australia and New Zealand was a coherent, generous, deliberate, and influential one.

2 'Alone with Shakespeare'

On her first and only visit to the southern hemisphere, Ellen Terry's programme was not of the lavish, full-scale performances of plays for which she had achieved fame with the Lyceum theatre in Britain and the United States. Instead, like many actresses before her in the latter phases of their careers, she developed a successful repertoire of solo performances. At the outset, however, the patching together of Terry's Shakespeare-themed addresses with comic entertainments by her manager and financial backer Joseph Blascheck seemed doomed. Some theatre critics and audiences found her lectures disappointingly derivative. Perhaps these factors alone have deterred scholarly curiosity. But a feminist perspective compels a reading less cowed by ageist discrimination and less committed to proper theatre and proper Shakespeare. In what became known as Terry's 'Lectures on Shakespeare', I posit a new stage in her evolution from 'actress' to woman theatre maker. To this end, the following section analyses the Shakespeare lectures (or 'discourses' as Terry preferred to call them) as a useful discursive space that Terry devised, not so much through writing as through performance. This was a space to which the time gap of age and the distance from England were an indispensable asset. It was in this space that she shaped a critique of the London stage, articulated her gender-political values, and produced new analytical commentary on Shakespeare in an age when this task was largely reserved for male scholars.

2.1 Travelling Light

In Section 1, I considered how the combination of Terry's age and chosen destinations has relegated her 1914 tour to the margins of scholarly curiosity. Here my focus is on the degree to which her chosen repertoire may have compounded this effect. Terry went to Australia, in Auerbach's words, 'alone with Shakespeare'.[59] In practice, this comprised an evolving programme of about two hours' duration which incorporated Terry performing parts of what were eventually published as Terry's *Four Lectures on Shakespeare* combined with dramatic and humorous 'acts' by her manager/tour backer/support act – Joseph Blascheck.

Before mocking this unseemly pastiche, we might reflect that such make-do mixed entertainments were more familiar to audiences of the era. In London during Terry's three-week season at the Savoy, her Shakespeare 'recital' was sandwiched between two short plays, one being J. M. Barrie's *Pantaloon*.[60] Even so, the eclectic assemblage of her touring programme drew criticism at first. The Melbourne-based social magazine *Table Talk* published a description of the first disastrous performances in the Melbourne Town Hall declaring that 'the mixed programme seems to be a mistake, for the people who wish to hear Miss Terry wish to hear her alone'. The acoustic properties of the space were ill matched to her intimate style of address and, to cap it all off, the audience mistakenly departed with the vice-regal party when the band played 'God save the King', thereby missing the second half of Terry's lecture.[61] Of Mr Blascheck's interludes, there is no description at all.

This picture of the opening night is grimly comic, with Blascheck playing multiple roles, including running on to tell the audience that it was not yet time to leave. It is given a full description in St John's introduction to the 1933 *Memoirs*. The episode reveals some of the risks Terry was courting by coming to Australia and New Zealand, 'alone with Shakespeare'. Although *Table Talk* goes on to praise the 'glimpse' of Terry's 'great powers', and to reveal her 'fascinating personality', and her 'quick, spontaneous wit', it is easy to see why

---

[59] Auerbach, *Ellen Terry*, p. 442.   [60] Terry, Craig, and John, *Ellen Terry's Memoirs*, p. 288.
[61] 'Miss Ellen Terry', *Table Talk*, 14 May 1914, p. 10.

a biographer reading this source might be tempted to confine the whole tour to an embarrassed footnote on Terry's artistic demise.

Yet, as previously observed, even before her biographers, Terry recognised the risk this version of herself potentially posed. She playfully deflected it, even as mishaps and misjudgements, illness and criticism conspired to confine her within it. The Terry and Blascheck combination, as laughable as it seems to us in retrospect, seemed to find its footing in the course of the tour, for together they went on to perform to acclaim along the Australian eastern seaboard and throughout New Zealand – a destination that all biographers leave out. Terry's Shakespeare lectures were undoubtedly the main attraction; media reports rarely mention Blascheck's support acts.

It is surprising, then, that the headline for Terry's final Melbourne performance on the 26th of October is 'Mr Blascheck's Recital', with the subheading 'Ellen Terry's Farewell'. In a more usual formulation, it describes the 'crowded', 'dramatic and humorous recital' as 'notable for the fact that Miss Terry made her last appearance in Melbourne'. It notes the presence of parties from Government House and 'Madame Melba' before going on to praise Terry's performance of Juliet's potion scene, and recital of poems by Suckling and Kipling. 'Mr Blascheck' is almost overlooked as being 'too well known in Melbourne to make description of his work necessary', but the journalist evidently thinks better of a complete dismissal:

> In the lighter vein his sketch of a Country J. P. was excellent [. . .] Ogilvie's 'Last toast', 'His first long trousers', a humorous extra 'Quick work', and Henry V exhorting his troops, and other pieces showed Mr Blascheck in a dozen moods and good in all of them.[62]

I will discuss Terry's capacity to play alongside performers of all kinds in Section 4, but in this programme, we get a glimpse of an artist much less concerned with protecting her reputation than some of her biographers have been. None of her letters imply condescension towards Blascheck or express frustration with the predicament of appearing alongside a performer whom many would view as her inferior. Instead, she seems to throw herself into the creative adventure with generosity. Perhaps she understood that she had more to gain in experience than to lose in reputation. She was evidently not particularly invested in the pretence of appearing as her younger self, but this is not a posture of defeat. Instead, her capacity to be who she was in the present created a narratively open space of time and distance which, through the course of her tour, Terry shaped into opportunity.

---

[62] 'Mr. Blascheck's Recital', *The Argus* (Melbourne: 1848–1957), 27 October 1914, p. 10.

Terry is not alone in theatre history as a female performer who creatively mined the gap between her former greatness as a Shakespeare star and her respected status as a veteran of the stage. In 1885 Helena Faucit (Lady Martin) published a book on eight of Shakespeare's female characters which was begun as letters to her dying friend and patron of the arts Geraldine Jewesbury.[63] Fanny Kemble and Charlotte Cushman added successful, later phases to their careers through Shakespeare readings in England and America.[64] Emma Stanley's 'Seven Ages of Woman' is another notable example of a touring show that exploited the internationally shared imaginary of Shakespeare's plays to forge new entertainments.[65]

In their minimal staging requirements, these solo shows bespeak artistic control. For this reason, it is wrong to see them as a diminished versions of the actresses' former repertoires or merely, as Manvell suggests, an opportunity to 'relive [...] greatest moments on stage'.[66] Touring acts such as the Shakespeare lectures merit attention for reaching wider and more diverse audiences than full-scale productions and for being more responsive to their performance contexts. In Ellen Terry's case, her Shakespeare 'discourses', as she insisted on calling them, were a canny device; they both capitalised on her fame as a star of the London stage and created a discursive and performative space in which she could evaluate and critique the conditions which had made it possible.

Capitalising on the idea of a long-deferred visit, Terry forged a conspiratorial bond with the Australian public by telling journalists she had 'always' wanted to visit Australia but that Henry Irving had prevented her:

> Miss Terry said that it had always been her desire to visit this country, but that she had never been able to realise her wish until now.
>
> 'Sir Henry Irving would always take every stick of furniture with him', she explained, 'and every actor in his company and all his own scenery, so you will see what a contract that would have been.'[67]

Terry's comment about being prevented in her wish to visit Australia by Henry Irving reinforces the idea that Australia and New Zealand were to receive a more authentic Terry, devoid of the trappings of her London stage career, reduced to simple and elegant props and costumes.

In an interview for *The Standard* before she departed London, Terry was asked what she would take. The New Zealand columnist 'Chryssa', for the Christchurch *Star*, eagerly relayed her response:

---

[63] Faucit, *On Some of Shakespeare's Female Characters*.

[64] Bratton, 'Frances Anne Kemble', pp. 120–32; Merrill, 'Charlotte Cushman', pp. 169–79.

[65] See Bratton and Bush-Bailey, 'Bodies of Evidence'.   [66] Manvell, *Ellen Terry*, p. 313.

[67] 'Not a Militant', *The Sun* (Sydney: 1910–1954), 13 May 1914, p. 9.

> I am going to take my own 'properties' with me to that great dominion
> beyond the seas; but they don't amount to much. Just a reading desk, my
> big book which has print expressly made to suit my treacherous eyesight, and
> my grey curtains.[68]

Reviews of Terry's performances rarely comment on her set or costume, implying that they were of little note. Even a column explicitly entitled 'Gossip for Women' gives a simple account:

> Each time she lectured she wisely chose a classically draped gown, her last
> one being a bright red robe in which the lines allotted to Portia seemed
> particularly appropriate.[69]

Terry's simple scheme of evocatively coloured classical robes implies her own acknowledgement that she was no longer 'playing' the roles. At the same time, it indicates a confidence that she herself – her own ideas and experiences – were the attraction (see Figure 4). Within Terry's beguiling conceit, antipodean audiences were to count themselves lucky to have, after a long wait, the liberated, intimate Terry. Terry gave her new audiences the Terry she could be now and nowhere else in the world but 'here'.

In the analysis of the lectures which follows, it becomes clear that the physical distance the lectures permitted her to gain from the London actor manager scene afforded her new intellectual and creative space. In this sense, Terry's tour to Australia and New Zealand in 1914 both represented and enacted a new form of creative agency. If Michael Booth's detailed analysis of Terry's creative reliance on pictorialism at the so-called 'height' of her career is accurate, then she was making an intrepid move into new territory by deciding to give lectures in Australia and New Zealand.[70]

2.2 The Dramaturgy of 'Discourse'

Before we examine the content of Terry's lectures, it is important to distinguish their life as performative 'discourses' from the published entity. While Terry's autobiography was published in her lifetime, her lectures were not. The 'lectures' were published in 1932, four years after Terry's death, appearing 'Edited with an Introduction by Christopher St John'. It is worthwhile observing that in this Introduction, which reveals a great deal about the working partnership and Terry's own creative processes, both Terry and St John express reservations about publication. St John states that Terry was 'opposed to their being made accessible in print, chiefly on the grounds that they had been

---

[68] 'For Women Folk', *Star* (Christchurch, NZ), 13 April 1914, p. 7.
[69] 'Gossip for Women', *The Week* (Brisbane: 1876–1934), 29 May 1914, p. 8.
[70] Booth, '*Ellen Terry*', pp. 83–4.

Figure 4 'Ellen Terry during her lecture tour', England, 20th century, © Victoria and Albert Museum, London. (Licence Purchased).

composed to be heard, not to be read', and St John, 'agreed that without the improvisations she made when she was lecturing, without the illumination of her ideas provided by her acting of the interpolated scenes, her lectures would be only half themselves'.[71]

---

[71] Terry, *Four Lectures on Shakespeare*, pp. 7, 8.

Despite this hesitation, the Shakespeare lectures were published and have been analysed as part of Terry's written legacy. Katharine Cockin, to whom we owe an enormous debt for insightful scholarship and for editing and publishing Terry's letters, analysed evidence that Terry employed St John to ghost-write the lectures and observed that negotiations between the two women over payment for this service were tense ahead of Terry's first lecture tour to America in 1910.[72] Conversely, Gail Marshall incorporates Terry's lectures as evidence of Terry's own authorship which freed her from the confining expectations associated with her reputation as an actress:

> In a way that was not possible within the complex mechanics of the Victorian spectacular stage, within which the actress was simply one component, Terry used her writing to assert a new dynamic of reading and of spectatorship which could exceed the heterosexual imperative of her on- and off-stage relationship with both Irving and her audiences.[73]

These insights are indispensable for understanding how the 'lectures' functioned as a written and later a published entity. However, St John's reservations and Terry's annotations make it important to read the literary artefact with a critical sensitivity to performance. The lectures were a dynamic intervention into the living moment, not a recitation of something Terry prepared in England and carried in her luggage. St John illustrates this: 'Not only did [Terry] make several different versions for different types of audiences; she gave each particular audience improvisations inspired by its response'.[74] Further, St John remarks upon the work Terry undertook in preparing them for performance – evident in the dense annotation of the script:

> Nearly every line in the copy she most frequently used is annotated by some instructions to herself about the way it should be spoken. 'Take time.' 'Quiet.' 'Keep still.' [...] 'With humour rather reckless.' [...] 'Dark, fierce, violent.'[75]

The context for which Terry prepared her lectures, and which went on to shape their evolution through performance, was not primarily England. Terry first conceived of the lectures in response to an invitation to address the Ladies' Theatrical Guild in Glasgow in 1903.[76] She performed them once in London and then with great success in America in 1910 and 1911. Returning to England, St John says, 'It was feared that even the magic of Ellen Terry's name would not draw the British public to a "lecture" [...]. So when Ellen Terry visited English towns, she was billed as appearing in "A Shakespearean Discourse with

---

[72] Cockin, 'Ellen Terry, the Ghost-Writer and the Laughing Statue', p. 60.
[73] Marshall, 'Ellen Terry: Shakespearean Actress and Critic', p. 362.
[74] Terry, *Four Lectures on Shakespeare*, p. 11.   [75] Ibid. p. 14.   [76] Ibid, p. 12.

Illustrative Acting" or in "A Shakespeare Recital."'[77] In 1912, a three-week season was successfully mounted at the Savoy in London – her 'recital' being sandwiched between two short plays.[78]

While Craig and St John were undoubtedly influential in the development of the script, they did not accompany Terry on her tours to America or Australia and New Zealand. St John explains that by the time Terry left for Australia her scripts had been utterly transformed from the original script with her own 'cuts', 'transpositions', and 'gags'.[79] On this evidence of Terry's working method, it is safe to assume that the discourses continued to evolve throughout her tour to Australia and New Zealand. What they were and what they became through performance must have been a concentrated effect of her personal connection with her audiences.

The performative characteristics of Terry's Shakespeare lectures are key to understanding their intervention into masculine domination of the Shakespeare imaginary and the professional stage. Katherine Kelly has observed how 'the lectures ... not only recorded retrospectively the subtext of Terry's principal Shakespeare roles but modelled women speaking on behalf of women at the threshold of the modern era'.[80] *Four Lectures on Shakespeare* (1932) expresses an unambiguous belief in gender equity and a partisan advocacy of changes to industry and legislation to better recognise the rights and capacities of women. As complex, situated performance events, Terry's lectures constituted a living critique of the institutions in which she had spent her life and achieved her greatest success. She uses the lectures to review her career and achieve the autonomy that she had surrendered in her years at the Lyceum. A good example of this is the moving disappointment she confides about having never played Rosalind:

> I have been Beatrice! Would that I could say 'I have been Rosalind'. Would that the opportunity to play this part had come my way in my prime! I reckon it one of the greatest disappointments of my life that it did not! In my old age I go on studying Rosalind, rather wistfully I admit.[81]

Marshall speculates that *As You Like It* was not included in Irving's Lyceum repertoire because it did not offer him a role as dazzling and dominant as it did Terry.[82] But if we are only reading the lecture on the page it is easy to lose sight of just how effectively Terry used the performative potential of the lecture to recover this lost opportunity. She exploits the special facility of performance as

---

[77] Terry, Craig, and John, *Ellen Terry's Memoirs*, p. 287.   [78] Ibid. p. 288.   [79] Ibid. p. 288.
[80] Kelly, 'The after Voice of Ellen Terry', p. 65.
[81] Terry, *Four Lectures on Shakespeare*, p. 97.
[82] Marshall, 'Ellen Terry: Shakespearean and Actress and Critic', p. 361.

a medium to *tell* what she has been prevented from doing and to *show*, at the same time, just how well she can do it.

Terry becomes Shakespeare's startling, wordy heroine; she plays both voices in the scene when Celia catches Rosalind despondent after they have watched Orlando wrestle:

CELIA　　　　[. . .] Is all this for you father?
ROSALIND　No, some of it is for my child's father.

To this tenor of cheeky intimacy Terry adds the voice of the tyrant uncle, banishing her from his court. Duke Frederick accuses Rosalind of treachery and Rosalind challenges, even commands him, to explain himself: 'Yet your mistrust cannot make me a traitor./ Tell me whereon the likelihood depends.' Then Terry intervenes to comment:

Now this is exactly what the Duke cannot do. So, beside himself with rage,
the rage of a man who knows he is wrong, he bellows out: 'Thou art thy
father's daughter: there's enough.'

Having 'bellowed' as the Duke, Terry includes a stage direction – in the published edition it is in italics but it is likely that she read it out: *Rosalind (with a touch of irony – my stage direction this!)*

So was I when your highness took his dukedom:
So was I when your highness banished him.

Terry's explanative commentary, her tonal 'touch of irony', amplifies the force of Rosalind's riposte which uses mirror sentences with strong iambic stress to point back to Frederick's treachery.

Although easy enough to read on the page, we can see that this is a punishingly complex feat of polyphonic performance. Katherine Kelly has registered many instances of praise for Terry's voice in the Australian and New Zealand reception: for her voice's 'modulations', 'changes', and range of 'intonation', and 'magnetic declamation'.[83] In these places, the preoccupation with speaking English 'properly' expressed in a rage for elocution training would have enhanced her appeal as an exemplar, and for emotional and tonal range and gesture, she could not have designed a better vehicle. In her lectures, which for reasons now apparent are better described as discourses, Terry set herself a challenge of switching between character and discursive modes. On the one hand, she positions herself as an actress playing multiple roles; on the other, she is critical commentator who links the fiction, as it unfolds, to her audience's real experience.

---

[83] Kelly, 'The after Voice of Ellen Terry', p. 71.

In her lectures Terry also performs herself as a feminist literary critic. There are four published lectures: 'The Children in Shakespeare's Plays', 'Shakespeare's Triumphant Women', 'Shakespeare's Pathetic Women', and 'The Letters in Shakespeare's Plays'. 'Letters in Shakespeare's Plays' breaks new ground through its designation of a topic new to scholarship, but the most popular lectures were the two on Shakespeare's women. Terry explains her resistance of the more conventional categories of 'tragic' and 'comic' and, within her newly devised framework, makes some novel claims – arguing that Lady Macbeth is a 'Pathetic Woman', and that Ophelia and Desdemona are much stronger than has been hitherto acknowledged by scholars. She arrogates a distinct kind of critical authority to herself, born of long professional experience as an actress:

> Please don't think that any 'theory' is implied in my classification. I leave theories to the scholars. An actress does not study a character with a view to proving something new about the dramatist who created it. Her task is to learn how to translate this character into herself, how to make its thoughts her thoughts, its words her words. It is because I have applied myself to this task for a great many years that I am able to speak to you about Shakespeare's women with the knowledge that can be gained only from union with them.[84]

Here we see that Terry ratifies her interpretative ideas through her practical experience and the affective force of her performance. Nothing she could say about Rosalind's courage or wit could persuade her audience if she could not also make those qualities felt in her performance.

As well as reconfiguring generic categories to suit her own actorly insight, Terry tackles head-on the chauvinistic staging conventions of the London theatre. In her 'Triumphant Women' lecture she mocks the stupidity of traditional stage business which reduced Beatrice in *Much Ado about Nothing* to petty jealousy. Speaking of a stage manager, Mr Lacy, engaged to assist Irving, she recalls that 'some traditional "business" [. . .] seemed so preposterous to me that I could hardly believe he really meant me to adopt it'. To illustrate her point, she quotes Mr Lacy's instruction: 'When Benedick rushes forward to lift Hero after she has fainted, you "shoo" him away. Jealousy, you see. Beatrice is not going to let her man lay a finger on another woman.' Terry then performs her past self in her defiant response: 'Oh nonsense, Mr Lacy!' If we imagine the dialogue with Terry adopting the voice of Lacy as she speaks his condescending advice, and then shifting to perform her own spirited come-back, we take a step closer to understanding the rhetorical mechanics of this hybrid form of entertainment and polemic. It is easy to imagine how the same words read aloud from

---

[84] Terry, *Four Lectures on Shakespeare*, pp. 84, 85.

the page by a 'nervy, restless' Ellen Terry, who was still recovering from her voyage at the beginning of her tour, could quicken to life when she began to speak from memory with playful confidence.

Evidently Terry had a deft ability to switch voice and demeanour to represent several characters in one scene. We see this in the way she incorporates the entire episode of fractious play between Beatrice and Benedick in Act 1, scene 1 of *Much Ado*. A reader of the published lecture may well glance over this scene because it is so familiar, but we should stop to consider what an extraordinary feat it is in performance. Within the complex discursive architecture of Terry's lecture, it takes on new significance:

> An ounce of practice is worth a pound of theory, so I will read one of the scenes in which the merry lady Beatrice and the merry gentleman Benedick cut and thrust at one another, making several palpable hits. The teasing merry lady begins the fencing bout:

BEATRICE	I wonder that you will still be talking, Signior Benedick: nobody marks you.
BENEDICK	What, my dear Lady Disdain! Are you yet living?
BEATRICE	Is it possible disdain should die while she hath such meet food to feed it as Signior Benedick! Courtesy itself must convert to disdain if you come in her presence.
BENEDICK	Then is courtesy a turncoat. But it is certain I am loved of all ladies, only you excepted; and I would I could find in my heart that I had not a hard heart; for truly I love none.
BEATRICE	A dear happiness to women: they would else have been troubled with a pernicious suitor. I thank God and my cold blood, I am of your humor for that: I had rather hear my dog bark at a crow than a man swear he loves me.
BENEDICK	God keep your Ladyship still in that mind: so some gentleman or other shall 'scape a predestinate scratched face.
BEATRICE	Scratching could not make it worse, an 'twere such a face as yours.
BENEDICK	Well, you are a rare parrot-teacher.
BEATRICE	A bird of my tongue is better than a beast of yours.
BENEDICK	I would my horse had the speed of your tongue and so good a continuer! But keep your way i' God's name. I have done!
BEATRICE	You always end with a jade's trick. I know you of old.

Here Terry plays a male character in conversation with a female character – embodying discourse, conflict, competition, and providing, through her performance skill, an existential instantiation of gender parity. Having performed the dialogue in their voices, Terry concludes, we might imagine a little out of breath: 'The result of this duel is a draw.'[85] She instantiates a battle of the sexes and lets it play out performatively so that its implications are felt before stated.

That audiences responded to Terry's affective force as a performer is without question. In the review quoted below, we get a sense of the quicksilver changes in her affective and embodied style of performance that far exceed what the word 'lecture' might convey:

> Again, Miss Terry's command of the art of gesture delighted everyone. Appeal, astonishment, persuasion, denunciation – all were shown in the use of her masterful hands, no less than in the subtleties of vocal inflection. The crescendos in the repeated, 'O that I were a man!' at the call to Benedick to punish Claudio for his wrongful accusation of Hero were admirable. All the men, she pointed out, believed this accusation at once (this was said with more than implied contempt in her tones), but Beatrice [...] showed her nobility by stoutly refusing to entertain any such suspicion. 'Indeed', the actress went on, 'she spoke out her mind like a man.'[86]

Terry used a combination of her past professional experience and her present performative force to command credibility for her original interpretations of the text and for the principles of gender equity and sociopolitical progress towards which they move.

Unfortunately, this dynamic quality of the 'discourses' as performance is ironed out when we treat them solely as part of her writing or as a posthumously published closed book of 'lectures'. Here I have attempted to examine them as an open discursive space which Terry was able to explore and expand in specific ways during her 1914 tour to Australia and New Zealand. The discursive adventure was as fraught with risk as the physical one: we see this writ large in the callous dismissal offered by the likes of John Norton in Section 1, in the shaky beginnings of her season at the Melbourne Town Hall, and in the seemingly laughable mismatch of Terry's material with Blascheck's.

These problems seemed solved when, as a published entity, *Four Lectures on Shakespeare*, achieved the stately poise befitting the reputation of England's national poet and England's great actress. We have good evidence, however, that Terry, when she left England to give the lectures in Australia and New Zealand, was seeking something else entirely; a new kind of conversation. This is evident in her mirthful resistance to the term 'lecture' and to the idea of acting in a conversation with a New Zealand journalist before she left London:

---

85 Ibid.   86 'Ellen Terry', *Darling Downs Gazette* (Queensland) 21 May 1914, p. 6.

> 'I shall not act in Australia', she said to a 'Standard' representative the other day. 'I shall just give my little comments on Shakespeare's heroines, interspersed with some of their most notable speeches, that misguided people will insist on calling my 'lectures.'[87]

By the time Terry reaches New York, after her time in Australia and New Zealand, her sense of humour is still intact and she seems even more archly assured about what she is (and is not) about. The Melbourne paper *Argus* reports from New York:

> [T]he gentlemen of the press [...] were ushered into Miss Terry's room, where they found her, sitting on the edge of her bed, and knitting something for the English soldiers to wear – if the war is prolonged long enough.
> 'You knit very well, Miss Terry', was the introductory remark of one of the reporters.
> 'Bless you for those kind, untruthful words. I cannot knit at all'.
> [...]
> 'Are you going to lecture here?' asked a reporter.
> 'Please don't say lecture – I hate the word; say "hold discourse" if you don't mind. Yes, I am, on Shakespeare.'[88]

3 'Permitted to be a person': Terry and Women's Suffrage

Terry's years at the heart of British theatre account in part for her appeal to antipodean audiences. Equally important for her Australian and New Zealand audiences was her emerging place at the forefront of the British fight for women's suffrage. Here I consider how Terry navigated the intersection of differently situated narratives of progress in the women's movement in Britain, Australia, New Zealand and the United States, and in turn the shaping influence these contexts had upon her own political rhetoric.

3.1 Playing the Suffrage Pioneer

A specific, informing context for the gender-political ambitions of Terry's Shakespeare lectures is The Pioneer Players, formed by Terry's daughter, Edith Craig, in 1911. The Pioneer Players had a mission to use drama to change the hearts and minds of the British population regarding the democratic rights of women. Craig unabashedly proclaimed its propagandist mission, saying that 'our plays take the place of tracts'.[89] Terry was appointed president of The

---

[87] 'For Women Folk', *Star* (Christchurch), 13 April 1914, p. 7.

[88] 'Miss Ellen Terry', *The Argus* (Melbourne: 1848–1957), 23 January 1915, p. 6.

[89] *Daily News and Leader* quoted in Cockin, *Women and Theatre in the Age of Suffrage*, p. 46.

Pioneer Players; her professional connections and years of public prominence were major assets to its political and artistic aspirations.[90]

As well as being a figurehead, Terry made an active creative contribution. In 1911 she played Nell Gwyn in Christopher St John's *The First Actress*, the very first production by the Pioneer Players. But playing actresses of the past was not new for Terry; in 1891 she had purchased the rights to Charles Read's *Nance Oldfield*, achieving commercial success by making the play and the character her own.[91] In 1909 she played Oldfield again in what Cockin has dubbed the 'explicitly political context' of the nationally touring production of Cicely Hamilton's *A Pageant of Great Women*.[92] Terry was a pioneer and played pioneers: she was a creative forerunner of women's professional autonomy and thereby embodied – even if she did not always expound – an argument for their political enfranchisement.

Terry's Shakespeare lectures distilled for Australian and New Zealand audiences the theatrical projects that formed such an important part of the British suffrage movement leading up to the Great War. Rather than seeing them as a throwback to her past career, there is good evidence that these female audiences saw Terry and her lectures as a living augmentation of a liberated and fully democratic present and future. The word 'pioneer' signals an imaginative rhetoric which reaches both backwards and forwards in time and space. This motif also structured Terry's Shakespeare lectures. As conceived by Terry, Shakespeare's 'triumphant' and 'pathetic' women were a pageant of exemplars of female courage and eloquent resistance to patriarchal oppression.

Like *The Pageant of Great Women*, the Shakespeare lectures push forward to political freedom for women by looking back to earlier ages. In them Terry argues that Shakespeare's heroines were the product of a culture with a more accurate understanding of female capabilities:

> Wonderful women! Have you ever thought how much we all, and women especially, owe to Shakespeare for his vindication of women in these fearless, high-spirited, resolute and intelligent heroines? Don't believe the anti-feminists if they tell you, as I was once told, that Shakespeare had to endow his women with virile qualities because in his theatre they were always impersonated by men! This may account for the frequency with which they masquerade as boys, but I am convinced that it had little influence on Shakespeare's studies of women. They owe far more to the liberal ideas about the sex that were fermenting in Shakespeare's age. The assumption that 'the woman's movement' is of very recent date – something peculiarly modern – is not warranted by history. There is evidence of its existence in the fifteenth century.[93]

---

[90] Cockin, *Women and Theatre in the Age of Suffrage*, p. 7.
[91] Cockin, 'Ellen Terry, the Ghost-Writer and the Laughing Statue', p. 155.   [92] Ibid. p. 155.
[93] Terry, *Four Lectures on Shakespeare*, p. 81.

Terry proceeds to speak in an informed way of educators Luis Vives and Erasmus and of female scholars and writers: Lady Jane Grey, Katharine of Aragon, and Mary Stuart. By historicising the 'woman's' movement, Terry suggests that impetus for the current struggle might be drawn from multi-generational lineage which spans real humans and fictitious inventions played by real actresses.

Terry and the triumphant and pathetic women of her Shakespeare lectures cut different figures against a different political landscape in Australia and New Zealand. In 1893 women in New Zealand had already achieved the vote; in 1902 women in Australia had achieved the right to vote and to run for parliament in federal elections.[94] In one sense Terry's lectures were a celebratory remnant of a narrative completed over a decade earlier; in another way they were a reminder to push forwards and consolidate steps in the direction of gender equality.

For the young women of New Zealand, Terry was evidently a living hero in a struggle for political change of which they were already beneficiaries. Her years at the Lyceum, far from being the faded zenith of her achievement, were, for these audiences, preparation for her ongoing broader vocation as a champion of women's suffrage:

> The great actress has been in the limelight now for many years, for she began at eight years old. So far as she is concerned, she has faithfully discharged her duties to her sex, and has never ceased her powerful advocacy of their true rights. Her life work has not been in vain. She has addressed three generations of men, and that with logic and power and irrefutable argument.[95]

Similarly, for the women of Australia, Terry, the mother of Edith Craig, functioned as a kind of ambassador for the British suffrage movement and its riven intensities post 1912. On her arrival in Sydney in May, journalists were curious about her exact stance and involvement in activism. Her quoted responses reveal the kinds of questions she was asked. 'Of course you all know I'm a suffragette', she announced with a mixture of pride and defiance. 'Of course I am, and so is my daughter, Edith Craig.' However, when asked about specifics, she uses self-effacing humour to evade the question:

---

[94] In New Zealand, women of mixed race who owned property freehold were eligible to vote in general seats in the federal election; Maori women voted in Maori electorates in December of 1893. Source: https://nzhistory.govt.nz/page/women-vote-maori-seats-first-time. In Australia the states made varied progress towards universal suffrage; in 1895 South Australia was the first electorate in the world to give equal voting rights to men and women. Australian Aboriginal men and women shared these rights: www.nma.gov.au/defining-moments/resources/indigenous-australians-right-to-vote.

[95] 'Ellen Terry', *Evening Post* (Wellington), 19 June 1914, p. 2.

> 'Have I ever walked in a procession?' she replied in answer to a persistent inquirer. 'Why, of course not. I wouldn't walk ten yards, much less in a procession.'

She nevertheless praises the 'glorious' bands of women who demonstrated in London on the 18th of November 1910 by comparing them to King Edward VII's 'tin-pot' funeral procession in May. She concentrates on how 'fresh' and 'tidy' they looked and avoids any reference to the violence perpetrated against them on what is now known as Black Friday.[96] Her trivialising equivocation continues:

> I am an ardent suffragette, but I don't believe in all their militancy. The suffragettes are a magnificent lot of women, but I think, perhaps, their ardour carries them away at times. And it shouldn't [...]. It makes them lose their poise, and poise is everything.

Terry refuses to reveal her thoughts on 'modern women', returning with the rhetorical quip: 'Why should I? I am both modern and old-fashioned myself.' The headline, 'Not a Militant. Ellen Terry – Suffragette. Arrival in Sydney. Breezy interview', distils the priorities of her Australian interviewers and her playful, seemingly superficial, approach to the serious matter of international women's suffrage.[97]

3.2 The Drama of British Suffrage

Australian journalists would have known that militancy was the dividing issue for the British movement for women's suffrage in 1914. Through her social status and emphasis on style, Terry would more readily be associated with the London-based, socially elite Pankhursts and their increasingly militant Women's Social and Political Union (WSPU) or 'suffragettes' than with the broader National Union of Women's Suffrage Societies (NUWSS) or 'suffragists' led by Millicent Fawcett who sought to distance themselves from violence. But Terry clings to the term 'suffragette' while denouncing militancy, making her hard to pin down. Her interviewer reinforces her slipperiness by physical description: 'She is never still a minute – even when she is doing what she calls "resting," her movements are as nervous and deliberate as a cat's.'[98]

This equivocation might have alienated Australian audiences, but instead, it seems to have mirrored a new ambivalence in Australian attitudes. Barbara

---

[96] 'Black Friday' is the name given to the occasion on which 300 protesters for women's suffrage, angered by the stalling of the progress of the Conciliation Bill, marched on the London Houses of Parliament and were subjected to police brutality which included many reported incidents of sexual assault. See Holton, 'Women's Social and Political Union (act. 1903–1914)'.

[97] 'Not a Militant', *The Sun* (Sydney: 1910–1954), 13 May 1914, p. 9.   [98] Ibid.

Caine has argued that many moderate Australian suffragists were galvanised into support for the militant faction when they themselves travelled to London from 1912 onwards – the period in which the WSPU was formed. There they came face to face for the first time with the dire social disadvantage experienced by women in a developed urban centre and with the rates of poverty, prostitution, and child prostitution. It also brought them within the domain of the mesmerising Pankhursts and their campaign which used costume and oratory of theatrical proportions for the cause.

Caine argues that Australian women, such as actress Muriel Matters, Vida Goldstein, and Bessie Rischbieth, were caught up in the 'drama' of the British suffrage movement which was reaching its zenith even as Australia broached a less spectacular challenge of applying newly won civil entitlements to political and social life:

> The contrast between English and Australian feminism was of course particularly marked at this point, as Australian women were grappling with the inevitable fragmentation that followed the granting of the suffrage and the attempt to establish what a female vote or a woman citizen might mean, while their English counterparts were in the throes of the most intense stage of their suffrage campaign.[99]

The suffrage banner created by Melbourne artist and activist Dora Meeson in 1908, and carried by a contingent of women from New Zealand and Australia at the Women's Suffrage Coronation Procession in London in 1911, reflects the complex dynamics of the relationship between the Australian and British movements in the first decade of the twentieth century (see Figure 5).[100] With a capitalised header 'Commonwealth of Australia', it depicts Australia as a young woman holding the Commonwealth Coat of Arms and coaxing a tall, proud looking Britannia to 'Trust the women mother, as I have done'. The banner on display in the art collection of Parliament House (Australia) reflects how Australia – annexing or negating New Zealand – understood itself as leading her 'mother' country towards enfranchisement of women. This figuration would have harmonised with the note of eager interest in young Australian and New Zealand women's questions directed to the tall and stately English veteran of the movement, Ellen Terry as she arrived by rail in their cities and towns and performed in their theatres and town halls. Regardless of her own ambivalence about activism, her presence stood in for an idea which they cherished; she was an ideal made flesh but a different ideal to the one with

---

⁹⁹ Caine, 'Australian Feminism and the British Militant Suffragettes'.
¹⁰⁰ Scott, *How Australia Led the Way*.

Figure 5 Dora Meeson (1869–1955) *The Women's Suffrage Banner*, 1908, Official Gifts Collection, Parliament House Art Collections, Department of Parliamentary Services, Canberra, ACT. Reproduced by permission of Lt Col. Simon Hearder on behalf of the heirs in copyright.

which she was primarily associated in England. Terry's presence might even have served as a chastisement to Australian complacency in a vein that Barbara Caine has identified:

> The dedication and the intensity of the suffragettes was also very attractive to
> Australian feminists, some of whom felt that their countrywomen were less
> engaged with their new rights and duties as enfranchised citizens than they
> should be.[101]

In any case it is very likely that in her shape-shifting pronouncements and
joking evasions, Terry allowed Australians with a wide range of political
opinions to believe she saw things as they did.

Just as Australian moderates became galvanised towards militancy through
their contact with London at the height of the movement, Terry's experience of
enfranchised Australia and New Zealand modified her understanding of the
struggle and the words which she chose to express it. In a letter written to Edith
between the 16th and 19th of June she is clearly troubled by the escalating
militancy of the campaign in the recent wake of the Westminster bombing (the
13th of June) and other attempted bombings in London, all of which were
reported in Australian newspapers:[102]

> Of, what <u>appears</u> *<u>to</u>* <u>me</u> the "*<u>set back</u>*" ['to me' and 'set back' are
> underlined twice] the Woman's Cause has suffered, I cannot speak either =
> mistaken energy surely & wanting to do too much in their <u>own day</u> –

She claims that her context has given her a new perspective:

> 'How poor are they that have not patience' – A long way from the scene of
> action I seem to see things clearer. Our present position surely is a <u>great strong</u>
> <u>link</u> in a chain which can scarcely be finished *<u>yet</u>* awhile – not of course in
> my time, altho' possibly??? It may be in yours? The magnificent fight should
> not have turned into vindictiveness on <u>our</u> part =

In daily company with women who had enjoyed the vote for over a decade, she
expresses confidence in the inevitability of triumph and attempts to reconcile
Australian criticism of Pankhurst and her own distaste for militancy with her
partiality towards 'our leader': 'Out here the fine women seem to think our Leader
should be changed. Poor Mrs Pankhurst! – She has certainly been crucified.'[103]
There is a stark contrast in tone between the serious conviction of her letters to
Edith and the retreat into self-effacing jokiness that seems to characterise her
press interviews. Evidently 'Being a long way from the scene' allowed Terry to
reflect upon the movement's internal contradictions and her own.

---

[101] Caine, 'Australian Feminism and the British Militant Suffragettes'.

[102] See for example 'The Suffragettes', *Weekly Times* (Melbourne: 1869–1954), 13 June 1914, p. 1.

[103] Terry and Cockin, *The Collected Letters* V6. (1745. 'To Edith Craig, 16–19 June [1914]'), p. 18.
Terry's use of underlining, strikethrough, the asterisk, the equals symbol, and other idiosyncratic punctuation and misspellings are reproduced here consistent with Cockin's presentation.
Terry frequently uses double underlining. Where this is relevant to note, it is indicated in square
brackets in the text.

In November the conservative Melbourne paper *The Argus* relays an interview that Terry gave to journalists in New York shortly after her arrival there on the 28th of November 1914. When asked if she is a suffragette, Edith is her touchstone: 'I refuse to discuss that question, but my daughter is an ardent one.' On the other hand, she delivers an apparently muddled verdict:

> I visited some place where the women had had suffrage for twenty years. [...] And I said to them, now that you have the vote what do you do with it? And one of them said: – 'Oh, I don't know, we meet and congratulate each other on it every day.' Amusing, is it not?[104]

Terry, as reported in this article, is an enigmatic figure. She might be aiming a blow at the political complacency of women in Australia and New Zealand; she might be expressing cynicism about women's suffrage movement altogether. The story certainly conspires at portraying Terry as endearingly 'disorientated'. Terry's maid, Bertha, supplies the name 'Australia', for the 'place' Terry is trying to recall; the correct name would have been 'New Zealand', the only place in the world in which, as Terry was surely aware, women had exercised suffrage rights for twenty years.

It is very difficult to say how much of this interview is a fabrication woven by journalists to amuse readers and how much is a true account. An appealing possibility is that Terry was strategically playing the old lady. None of her interviews in Australia and New Zealand indicate such dithering absent-mindedness, and it seems unlikely that a woman who remembered the name 'Toowoomba' after passing it on a train would have forgotten the name of the country she had taken such pains to visit, where she had recuperated, and had lectured in at least eight locations across two islands. Her convincing per-formance of forgetful old age would have created a convenient cover from which to gauge the political climate in a context in which women's suffrage was yet to be won.

Having once acclimatised to America, however, Terry seems to express deeper conviction in her political beliefs than ever before and makes more explicit links between her creative work and her political orientation. By the time she reached Virginia in January of 1915, her lecture content was framed unashamedly as a vehicle for her political views:

> Terry has advised that she expects to arrive in Harrisburg this evening in time to attend House of Representatives to hear a lecture by the United States Senator Moses E. Clapp who will speak under the auspices of the

---

[104] 'Miss Ellen Terry', *The Argus* (Melbourne: 1848–1957), 23 January 1915, p. 6.

Pennsylvania State Women's Suffrage Association. Miss Terry is an enthusiastic suffragette, the truly English kind, and in her interpretations of the various roles of Shakespearean heroines, she asserts that she finds in each of them, all the attributes of the modern suffragette.[105]

Speaking of Shakespeare's heroines Beatrice, Rosalind, and Portia, Terry is reported as saying, 'Surely, they would all be suffragists today, and may be suffragettes.'[106] The implicit treatment of the characters as real historical persons is informative. As characters they have always relied on performers for embodied interpretation and as the authoritative British actress who plays these parts, Ellen Terry implicitly positions herself as the evidence for her own argument.

4 'Australia is a garden': Terry and Melba

Influenced by the documented gloomy predictions of Terry's friends and family, scholars have hitherto emphasised the hardship and even martyrdom of her 1914 tour to Australia and New Zealand. There is no doubt that Terry was dogged by illness and anxiety about the war during her tour. Her letters reveal that her travel plans were frequently interrupted, her performance schedule scuttled, and that she eventually abandoned the most direct route home – via the Red Sea and Suez canal – because her doctor advised that her heart might not sustain exposure to the heat that she had endured on the way to Australia. We also see that correspondence was disrupted by the war, contributing further to Terry's sense of helplessness and isolation. She was, on occasions, near despair about her return and about the gravity of the situation at home.

It follows that most accounts of Terry's tour to Australia and New Zealand skip over her positive evaluation of it, expressed here, towards its conclusion, in a letter to her friend Graham Robertson:

> It wd I suppose have been wiser at my time of [life] to stay home, but I <u>cannot</u> repel the beauty of the journey, for the beauty of <u>Colombo alone</u>, will dwell with me for ever & I have met with a few fine souls, & received much kindness. Also I have picked up some gold & silver (not <u>much</u> but) which will <u>come in</u> usefully at home & I have heard Nelly Melba sing The Blackbird – !! = just to <u>me</u> – alone "&so – come death" ("Dies to <u>slow music</u>") *No* – <u>Lives</u> to <u>joyous</u> music.[107]

---

[105] 'Ellen Terry Will Hear Senator Clapp', *Harrisburg Telegraph*, 26 January 1915, p. 4 (Terry missed this event because her train arrived too late).

[106] 'Amusements', *Harrisburg Telegraph*, 18 February 1915, p. 4.

[107] Terry and Cockin, *The Collected Letters* V6. (1755. 'To Graham Robertson, 9 October 1914'), p. 32.

Terry lists among her experiences several that made it all worthwhile. Among these were encounters with extraordinary natural beauty of locations visited and friendship with the Australian opera star Nellie Melba. In this section, I demonstrate how these two mitigations to the hardships of her tour were linked, and that Terry's capacity to take comfort and inspiration from her human and natural surroundings was a result of her culturally literate openness to place.

4.1 Worry and Wonder

In Section 3, I noted how Terry's expressed affinities with the political scene in Australian and New Zealand mitigated potential for a negative reception. The exuberance of Terry's publicly expressed admiration for Australia and New Zealand's distinctive natural environments likewise chimed with the way European settler communities sought to understand themselves as young and full of promise. Despite what we know of her illness, newspaper commentary suggests she was very successful in projecting a youthful energy in response to her surroundings. On disembarking her train from Sydney to Brisbane on the 20th of May, a journalist reports that

> [a]ge, relentless in the pursuit of most people, has failed to depress the wonderful spirits and ardour of this remarkable woman, who, to use her own words, 'feels as young as a child'.[108]

The reporter expects her to be exhausted after her twenty-eight-hour journey from Sydney, but instead Terry is quoted marvelling at the landscape she has traversed, recalling local place names with accuracy and noticing fine details in the flora:

> 'What glorious scenery that is just past Toowoomba', she said, 'and the railway itself. What a wonderful feat of engineering. I was fascinated by the foliage of the trees too, so different from what I have seen before. Australia is a beautiful country.'[109]

It would be easy to dismiss Terry's enthusiastic response to Australia as a mere public relations campaign if it were not so closely echoed in her private communication. Writing to Edith Craig en route from Fremantle to Melbourne she exclaims, 'It is all the deepest blue sky I see & the Southern Cross like a great Jewels [*sic*] laid out across the blue'. She describes some flowers that were sent to her from Melbourne: 'amazing flowers – yellow tangle <u>of small</u> Orchids' – Great <u>blue</u> <grey white> and yellow) Water Lillies & some deliciously scented Roses

---

[108] 'Ellen Terry', *Daily Standard* (Brisbane: 1912–1936), 21 May 1914, p. 6.

[109] 'Ellen Terry in Town', *The Telegraph* (Brisbane: 1872–1947*)*, 21 May 1914, p. 8.

(emphasis original)'.[110] Notice how Terry's idiosyncratic punctuation markings strain to capture her ecstatic delight.

Throughout her whole correspondence, whether she reports being sick or well, cheerful in company, or anxious to be home, there is an appetite to learn about her surroundings. Prior to her visit to Australia an Adelaide publication called 'The Journal' includes a London correspondent's interview with her in which she says: '[T]hat's what I want to see – that strange Australian bush of which I have read and heard so much.'[111] On her arrival in Brisbane on the 20th of May, Terry is reported saying, 'I would love to live near the real bush and seek adventure – I'm only a girl really after all.'[112] Her use of the word 'bush' in a statement to the press demonstrates her sensitivity to Australian vernacular. In a letter dated the 30th of July, Terry uses the word 'bush' with a capital 'B' and in quotation marks, signalling her awareness that it was a local word. Had she used the word 'woods', or 'forest', her sentiments would have served only to mark her difference. By using the term 'bush' and expressing her anticipation to experience it, Terry naturalises herself.

Making the arduous crossing from Sydney to Auckland from the 27th to the 31st of May, Terry's response to the New Zealand landscape reflects similar eager anticipation and affinity:

> I like your climate, and I am charmed with New Zealand. [. . .] I love the grandeur
> of your mountains and the wild, rugged scenery – it is beautiful. I was very ill
> coming over, but I would not have missed seeing New Zealand for anything.
> I undertook the trip partly for health reasons and already I feel much better.[113]

Here we see that she experiences the beauty of her surroundings as a direct mitigation of her illness. Terry rested for about a week in the geothermal resort town of Rotorua on arriving in New Zealand before continuing a hectic schedule of engagements on both the North and South Islands.

Returning to Sydney, it appears that Terry experienced a new bout of illness, evinced by a letter she addresses from Jenner Private Hospital (at Potts Point in Sydney). Nevertheless, her spirits are sustained by the view from her window which she describes as

> every lovely dream & picture of combined sea, mountain, cloud, a lovely part
> of the city amongst trees & 'Bush' on the spur of a hill leading down into the
> Pacific.[114]

---

[110] Terry and Cockin, *The Collected Letters* V6. (1740. 'To Edith Craig, 30 May–5 April [1914]'),
       p. 11.

[111] 'When I Was a Girl', *The Journal* (Adelaide: 1912–1923), 2 May 1914, p. 6.

[112] 'Woman's World', *The Brisbane Courier* (Qld.: 1864–1933), 21 May 1914, p. 9.

[113] 'A Charming Personality', *North Otago Times*, 13 July 1914, p. 6.

[114] Terry and Cockin, *The Collected Letters* V6. (1748. 'To Edith Craig, 30 July, [1914]'), p. 22.

As Australian autumn passes into winter, and the world lurches towards war, Terry's letters home reflect increasing alarm about her loved ones and her thwarted attempts to return home. It is remarkable then that, rather than detaching herself from the place she seeks to leave, she takes sustenance from its natural beauty. One letter dated early in the Australian winter is entitled 'Beronia', [*sic*] and describes in loving detail that small, fragrant, west Australian flower. In late July, when only the very earliest Wattle flowers would have been in bloom, Terry has already noticed them:

> Wattle is the national flower & is like Mimosa (of a very large kind) very softly beautifully ~~yellow~~ golden, & with strange dream-y <u>silver</u> leaves of a flat shape.[115]

None of this is intended to negate the fact, observed by all of Terry's biographers, that Terry's hardships during her tour were dire and multiple. The health conditions Terry mentions include diarrhoea, weight loss, breathing difficulties, weakness and fatigue, diminishing vision, and a diagnosed heart complaint. In an early letter home addressed to Christopher St John 'from my bed, The Australia', her upmarket hotel in Sydney, Terry's health conditions cast an ambivalent shadow over her destination. Will Australia atone for the struggle she has endured to reach and traverse its vast distances?

> I have been too ill to write or read or go anywhere, & how I have stood up straight & gone through with the Lectures Lord knows – The journeys by ship & train have nearly killed me. [. . .] 'God's own Country' they call this – I confess I've only seen it so far from a <u>bed</u> ['bed' is underlined twice] in my room = Certainly I've never seen so much Sun shine – & it is fairly cool at the same time – but <u>as yet</u> – well! // I'm a <u>good</u> deal changed – very thin[.][116]

Poignantly, in this early letter she is already eager to return home. Little did she know it was to be a year before she would see England again.

Terry's erratic state of health was compounded by the inability to receive word from home on a regular basis. Evidently, she received no news from home while in Fremantle or on landing in Melbourne, and she craves any news at all from England or about England.[117] In a letter addressed to Edith from Wellington on the 19th of June, Terry wishes she could have heard from her, having received only one letter.[118] On the 30th of July she writes to Edith optimistically: 'Whether the War will stay traffic by Sea I don't know – but maybe it will turn out only a Paper war.' She is playful in expressing her

---

[115] Ibid. (1748. 'To Edith Craig, 30 July [1914]'), p. 14.
[116] Ibid. (1741. To [Christopher St. John]), Tuesday, 26 May [1914]), p. 14.
[117] Ibid. (1740. To [Edith Craig], 30 April–5 May [1914]), p. 10.
[118] Ibid. (1745. To [Edith Craig], 16–19 June [1914]), p. 16.

disappointed hopes of receiving a letter from her daughter: 'I shot ~~an Arrow~~ a letter into the air it fell to earth I know not where – I never seem to hear from you. Mother.'[119] On the 6th of August the terrible realisation has dawned that the war will make 'all sorts of difference to the back- & forthing of the Ships!' but Terry still hopes to depart as intended from Perth on the 20th of October. By late August Terry's fears about the impact of the war in Europe have become vivid. In a letter to Edith titled 'Melbourne = <u>25 August – Very cold Lovely!</u>' she writes:

> My darling – As there's <u>more</u> than a chance this will never reach you, I shall say but little – <u>All my love to you</u> – By to days [*sic*] papers it seems to <be> likely enough <that> the Germans have <u>raged</u> through the beautiful little Bruges, and maybe are even in Kent! – perhaps are inhabiting <u>our Cottages!</u> & – perhaps you may be giving them some Tea! [...] The horrors of of [*sic*] this War for a few ~~minutes~~ minutes now & again make me crazy – when I dare <u>think</u> – but I daren't – & only pray no harm comes near you, & that <u>somehow</u> <u>or another</u> we meet at home before Xmas.[120]

The anxiety of posting this letter into anticipated oblivion is reflected in the strange underlining and the fearful, fidgety tone: now loving and anxious, now playful, now wistful. Another source of strain appears in mid-August in a letter to the husband from whom she was amicably separated, James Carew: not only is she despondent about her plan to return but performances have been cancelled:

> I can't get away from here now until 3rd November – <u>p'raps</u> not then! = This terrible War has knocked all business into a cocked hat, and many, including myself, have had to cancel all dates of <u>small</u> places ...[121]

Cut off from loved ones, consumed with anxiety for their safety, and even unable to continue to earn income, Terry seems to have met her darkest moment.

4.2 Friendship and Recovery

Despite Terry's grim prospects of profit or a safe return home, another, brighter thread of feeling starts to weave its way through her correspondence at about this time. It is echoed in what we see in newspaper reporting and seems to lend her newfound strength and to aid in her physical recovery. Leaving her planned repertoire behind, Terry begins to work with other Australian actors, and the bonds she forms with them are evidently invigorating.

---

[119] Ibid. (1748. To [Edith Craig], 30 July [1914]), p. 22.
[120] Ibid. (1752. To [Edith Craig], 25 August [1914]), p. 27.
[121] Ibid. (1750. To James Carew, 16 August [1914]), p. 2.

The Actors' Association of Australia organised a benefit concert for Terry at Her Majesty's Theatre in Sydney on the 28th of July. On this occasion she performed as Portia in the trial scene in *The Merchant of Venice*. In a letter to Edith on the same day she writes,

> 8-oclock – evening –
> Very tired – all went well. Big house – wished you there
> Off to bed = from my bed I see the lovely Sydney Harbour all lighted up.[122]

In a letter to Edith dated the 30th of July, she returns to this theme, 'the big Matinee on 28th a great success in the way it was managed & received'. She then describes performances by other actors and concludes, 'Miss Essie (!) Jermyns [*sic*] was nice', and 'there was nearly £700 in the house.'[123]

Essie Jenyns was the much-loved actress credited with inspiring a Shakespeare revival in Australia through her portrayal of Shakespeare's heroines in the penultimate decade of the nineteenth century.[124] She had married and left the stage in 1888, so her return at the age of fifty to play Nerissa opposite Terry's Portia was a cause for great local excitement. There is little doubt that the combination of Terry and Jenyns made the event doubly attractive to audiences:

> The association of England's most famous Shakespearean actress of modern times, with Australia's greatest Shakespearean actress in the performance of the Trial scene from the 'Merchant of Venice' at Her Majesty's Theatre in Sydney next Tuesday afternoon is a unique and historic event in the theatrical world.[125]

Inevitably, the event also drew negative attention:

> The Ellen Terry matinee given by the Actors' Association was a huge success for Ellen. The place was packed at record prices, so Ellen will have a nice fat cheque in addition to the illuminated souvenir programme and the adulation and cheers which were hers on the great afternoon. Ellen played 'Portia' in the trial scene from 'The Merchant of Venice' and Essie Jenyns appeared as 'Nerissa.' It was not a great show, but it was vastly amusing, especially when Ellen kissed Essie and Essie kissed Ellen.[126]

John Norton, the author of the vicious attack in *Truth* (see Section 1), deems the ticket price extortionate, the takings undeserved, and makes a mockery of the demonstrations of warmth between the two mature actresses. Nevertheless,

---

122 Ibid. (1747. To Edith Craig, 28 July [1914]), p. 21.
123 Ibid. (1748. To Edith Craig, 30 July [1914]), p. 22.
124 Van Der Poorten, 'Jennings, Elizabeth Esther Helen (1864–1920)'.
125 'Two Actresses', *The Sydney Morning Herald* (NSW: 1842–1954), 25 July 1914, p. 8.
126 'Sydney Snapshots', *Truth* (Brisbane: 1900–1954), 9 August 1914, p. 12.

the event remained a bright spot in Terry's memory; on the 6th of August, she writes to Edith:

> I don't know whether I told you of the splendid Performance the actors gave me in Sydney[.] I can't tell you of it now – but it was all extraordinarily enthusiastic and kind of them – altho' I cant [*sic*] face <u>writing</u> much – I am <u>really better.</u>

The mind reflected in Terry's writing jumps fitfully from subject to subject leaving the connections unclear, but here it is likely that she links her recovery to friendship with other actors.

Evidently Terry turned her energies towards more collaborative and charitable endeavours throughout the second half of her visit. Two 'Patriotic Matinees' at Her Majesty's Theatre in Melbourne are announced in Melbourne *Punch* for the 28th of August – one in the morning and one in the afternoon:

> All the companies at present playing, as well as several artists who chance to be here, are willing to give their services, as also are the stagehands and employees of her Majesty's.

Ellen Terry's appearing as Portia *and* giving her 'lecturette' on *The Merchant of Venice* heads an eclectic list including acts by actors, singers, comedians, and even a 'a naval tableau of the deck of the Dreadnought'.[127] The excitement attendant upon this rallying for a cause – the mingling in the crowded green room – would have been less demanding and more stimulating than Terry's usual programme. It is not difficult to imagine that this was reinvigorating.

4.3 Madame Melba

The day after Terry sailed from Sydney for Vancouver, the *Sydney Morning Herald* reported that

> Miss Terry expressed herself as being delighted with her visit to Australia and New Zealand, and with her holiday in retirement with Madame Melba. Of all the towns she has visited, she says her sweetest remembrances will be those of Sydney, and the great kindness showered upon her by her brother and sister actors and actresses there.[128]

No doubt the *Herald* was making the most of an opportunity to gild the occasion, promoting idyllic bonds formed between Terry and her Australian counterparts to promote Australian talent as not beneath the notice of the British Shakespeare star. Fortunately, there is an abundance of evidence to help us test,

---

[127] 'The Patriotic Matinees', *Punch* (Melbourne.: 1900–1918; 1925), 27 August 1914, p. 44.
[128] 'Miss Ellen Terry's Departure', *The Sydney Morning Herald* (NSW: 1842–1954), 30 October 1914, p. 5.

at the very least, the claim that Madame Melba's company and hospitality had a restorative influence on Terry and would be remembered fondly by her.

On the 15th of August *The Australasian* reports that Nellie Melba, freshly returned from London, received a letter from Ellen Terry offering to assist at her planned concert in aid of the Red Cross Society.[129] The following day, Terry writes to James Carew that plans to work with Melba are already afoot and that she has enjoyed a visit with Melba at her country estate, Coombe Cottage:

> Melba is going to give a big performance for the War Fund in about 3 weeks [*sic*] time = I assist at that Show – I spent a few days with her at her lovely home <near> here – about 30 miles by Motor – It is among the [. . .] Hills – a little Palace called Coombe Cottage! = She is very jolly and kind – her son & his wife live there.[130]

Anticipating this performance and another visit to Coombe Cottage only about ten days later Terry writes to Edith on the 25th of August that

> Melba too gives a big performance & I help – & then go to stay with Melba at her wonderful fairy home amongst the Wattle, and the Blue Mountains = how she loves it – seems <u>half</u> her age, & gleesome as a Kitten.[131]

Here a new note makes itself heard in Terry's correspondence. Amid anxiety are distinctive themes of pleasure, friendship, and anticipatory excitement. Over the successive two months Terry enjoyed multiple visits to Melba's rural property in the Yarra Valley and together they turned their energies towards the war effort and other local causes, appearing in at least four highly publicised charity events. Earlier work has remarked on the encouragement and support Terry drew from her friendship with Melba, but to date, this bond between exceptional women has attracted no detailed scholarly attention.[132] Terry's erratically capitalised reference to 'the Blue Mountains' has led to some confusion. It is quite clear Terry intended this as descriptive of the Dandenong Ranges and not as a place name. Melba's Coombe Cottage is in rural Victoria (now part of greater Melbourne), while the Blue Mountains are 60 kilometres west of Sydney, over 880 kilometres away.

One effect of this alternating schedule of retreat and collaborative activity seems to have been Terry's sustained recovery. Reporting on Terry's appearance at Melba's 'big performance' on the 10th of September, the Melbourne

---

[129] 'Personal', *The Australasian* (Melbourne: 1864–1946), 15 August 1914, p. 29.

[130] Terry and Cockin, *The Collected Letters* V6, (1750. To James Carew, 16 August [1914]), p. 24.

[131] Terry and Cockin, *The Collected Letters* V6, (1752. To Edith Craig, 25 August [1914]), p. 27.

[132] Both Cockin and Manvell mention Terry's visits to Melba; Cockin sees the friendship as salutary; see Cockin, 'Introduction', in Terry and Cockin, *The Collected Letters*, V6. p. xiv; and Manvell, *Ellen Terry*, p. 315.

women's magazine *Table Talk* celebrates 'a peep of Miss Ellen Terry as she really is … such a different Ellen Terry to the poor, sick wraith of herself we heard previously in Melbourne'.[133] Likewise, *The Bendigo Advertiser* reports that

> Miss Ellen Terry [...] is quite a different woman to what she was when she last appeared here. She walks on the stage briskly, and holds herself as if she has some strength, while her voice is strong and firm. If she had only been like this when she gave her recitals it would have been very different as regards her success. But it was really painful to listen to her and watch her then.[134]

Terry had a second chance to impress her Melbourne audiences, and she made the most of it. This evident turnaround troubles the version of Terry's tour to Australia and New Zealand as an undifferentiated period of exile, failure and disappointment. We see, if we look more closely, that the networks Terry had begun to forge with other actors, and particularly the friendship, hospitality, and professional collaboration she and Melba extended to one another, transformed her experience of Australia and, by extension, Australian audiences' experience of her.

In what remains of this section, I uncover some delightful details of the warm professional attachment between Terry and Melba. In doing so, I hope to bring into view a clear example of the new feminist geography emergent in the first generation of international women theatre makers. I speculate on how the many parallels between Terry's and Melba's life experience might have strengthened their bond and analyse extant evidence to offer a clearer picture than has yet been provided of how they spent their time together.

4.4 Family, Fame, and Scandal

Terry and Melba's eminence as female global celebrities entailed much shared experience that was otherwise rare for women in their era. Terry, beginning her career with the internationally recognised Charles and Ellen Kean at the Princess Theatre in London, had gone on to wider fame as the partner of Henry Irving at the Lyceum theatre. Shakespeare was central to her repertoire throughout this period and to the multiple tours the Lyceum made to America. After Irving's death, Terry turned to theatre management and sought to bring the modern works of Ibsen and Shaw to the English stage. At the time of her visit to Australia, she had also already published her autobiography and was involved with the feminist Pioneer Players, as previously discussed.

---

[133] 'The Ladies Letter', *Punch* (Melbourne: 1900–1918; 1925), 24 September 1914, p. 40.
[134] 'Melbourne Social Notes', *Bendigo Advertiser* (Vic.: 1855 – 1918), 17 September 1914, p. 4.

Nellie Melba, by 1914, had attained a stratospheric level of career success and fame. Notably, in all the press concerning their collaborative endeavours, it is Melba's name that comes first. Perhaps the most famous opera singer of her era, she was fourteen years Terry's junior, but unlike Terry, she was not born to a career in entertainment. As Helen Porter Mitchell, she showed early promise in elocution and music while studying at the Presbyterian Ladies College in Melbourne. When her mother and sister died in 1880, her father removed the family to the small north-eastern Queensland town of Mackay. There, in 1882, she met and soon married Charles Armstrong – a man of landed aristocratic heritage who was three years her senior.

Two years later Nellie 'Armstrong' made the decision that would set her life on its extraordinary course. Shortly after the birth of her first child, George, she returned to Melbourne to continue her musical training with the teacher Pietro Cecchi.[135] Throughout his childhood, George evidently travelled with his mother, and by the time Terry visited her at Coombe Cottage, adult George and his wife were living there with her. This arrangement would have echoed Terry's life at home in England. On her country property referred to as the 'Farm' in Kent, she lived in the main house – Smallhythe – and gave the cottage, called 'Priest's house' to Edy and Chris. Auerbach describes Edith's work to make a garden for her mother there.[136]

Thus, by 1914, both Terry and Melba were owners of small country estates, which were also home to their adult children and their partners. Photographs and footage of Melba and Terry at their respective properties indicate an idyllic lifestyle; the much-loved matriarchs are often pictured out of doors and surrounded by children, grandchildren and favourite animals. See for example the image of Ellen Terry at https://commons.wikimedia.org/wiki/File:Ellen-Terry-and-Granddaughter.jpg. This goes some way to explaining why Terry felt such comfort at Coombe Cottage and in the company of Melba. However, these unusual arrangements also reflect the unconventionalities of both women's relational histories and hint at more turbulent personal pasts. Both Terry and Melba had experienced the precarity of mothering young children outside of the conventional family unit while working in a demanding industry. Melba had left her home and husband with her small son to pursue her career. Terry had both her children, Edith and Edward, to the architect Edward William Godwin, with whom she had eloped while still legally married to the painter George Frederick Watts. Watts had married sixteen-year-old Terry when he was forty-six.

---

135 'A Geebung Goddess', *Truth* (Sydney: 1894–1954) 16 June 1901, p. 3.
136 Auerbach, *Ellen Terry*, p. 370.

While early marriage introduced a long pause to Terry's career, Melba had pursued hers doggedly. In 1886, as Ellen Terry and Henry Irving saw their meteoric rise to fame at the Lyceum Theatre, Melba accompanied her father on a business trip to London where she began to test her powers as an opera singer but with little success. She then auditioned in Paris for Mathilde Marchesi, who became her teacher and recommended that she change her name.[137] Melba chose the name by which she became known as a tribute to her home city of Melbourne. Paris and Brussels proved fertile grounds for Melba's further artistic development, and through attendance at several salons, her singing was refined, and her reputation began to strengthen. She established herself in the roles of Gilda in *Rigoletto*, Violetta in *La Traviata*, and Lucia di Lammermoor; success came with her breakthrough performance in *Romeo et Juliette* for the Royal Opera at Covent Garden, London, in 1889.[138] In 1914, just before war broke out in Europe, Melba returned to Australia from the most recent of many triumphant seasons playing Mimi in Puccini's *La Boheme* at the Royal Opera, Covent Garden. During her time in London, Melba and Henry Irving must have crossed paths, for an Australian newspaper notes that he had described her as 'the incomparable Nellie Melba' in her autograph book.[139]

In 1890, Melba had met Philippe Duke of Orleans, with whom she evidently began an affair, the public nature of which, mediated by newspapers, precipitated her divorce. Armstrong took his young son George back to America, where he was living, and Philippe went on a two-year African safari, leaving Melba doubly bereft.[140] This relationship and its demise in 1895 were the subject of gleeful derision by John Norton, the Australian satirist who cruelly mocked Terry, as previously noted:

> That giddy young Don Juan, the Duke of Orleans, has at length fallen in and has been made co-respondent in a divorce suit, shortly to be heard in London. It will be remembered that some time ago his name and that of Madame Melba were somewhat freely associated, so freely in fact that the lawful husband of the lady attempted to pull the ducal nose out by the roots, and was desirous of fighting Orleans in any style or with any weapon, from pop-gun to wood-axe. The Frenchman wasn't on. He has been in several similar scrapes in the last few years and his family has urged him to go to Utah and turn Mormon. He, however, prefers to remain in Europe and enjoy the stolen kisses in which his soul (if he has one) delights.[141]

---

[137] The intensity of Melba's affiliation with her home country and city is reflected in the fact that she took on the name 'Melba' as an echo of Melbourne; see Davidson, 'Melba, Dame Nellie (1861–1931)'.

[138] Davidson, 'Melba, Dame Nellie (1861–1931)'.

[139] 'His Last Cup', *Worker* (Brisbane: 1890–1955), 18 June 1914, p. 12.

[140] Davidson, 'Melba, Dame Nellie (1861–1931)'.

[141] 'The Critic', *Truth* (Sydney: 1894–1954), 3 November 1895, p. 1.

Norton stops short of launching a direct attack on Melba – wise given the stature of her popularity at the time – but it is not difficult to see the sideways insult he administers: that she has too 'freely' associated with a philandering European dandy for whom she is only one among the many women he has seduced. Norton perseveres in bringing this point home in another reference the following year, this time in a section of his paper entitled 'Corner Chronicles': 'The frisky little Duc d' Orleans who caused such a fuss in the Melba household, is now trotting around with Mme Calve, the magnificent millionaire nightingale.'[142]

In other pieces focusing on Melba, Norton excoriates her for lack of gratitude to Cecchi – her Melbourne singing teacher – for affectation, egotism, coldness, and lack of generosity. In 1901, just prior to her first major return tour of Australia, he accuses her of breaking many promises to make the tour and of requiring extortionate fees for her performances. If his accounts are correct – and they seem in keeping with other records – she turned down an offer of £400 per performance with all expenses paid, claiming that in London she was paid twice the sum. Certainly, Melba's talent came with a very high asking price, but we have to reflect on whether a male performer of her calibre would have been mocked in the following manner:

> Nellie Mitchell, afterwards Mrs Armstrong, and subsequently and at present Madame Melba, cares not a fig about Australia or Australians[143]

The history of Melba's names is extraneous to the point Norton makes here, but by listing them, he reminds readers of her complicated relational past and paints her as a slippery egotist. As we shall see, Melba's modern legacy, shaped by her energetic support of the war effort, the delight she brought to her local town and surrounds, and her subsequent philanthropy, makes it easy to forget such scathing judgements levelled at her earlier in her career.

Both Terry and Melba had sailed the waves of private grief and public scandal. By 1914 most of the press portray them as elegant dowagers whose connection with one another was highly celebrated and ratified their respectability, but it is unlikely they had forgotten the years of sniping criticism. Did they confide private scars, doubts, and regrets in one another? It is at least possible that the bond between Terry and Melba was strengthened not only by present success but by the shared threat they had weathered for decades of a pointedly gendered discourse of public scorn.

---

[142] 'Corner Chronicles', *Truth* (Sydney: 1894–1954*)*, 17 May 1896, p. 2.
[143] 'A Geebung Goddess', *Truth* (Sydney: 1894–1954) 16 June 1901, p. 3.

4.5 'Touring with Mme Melba'

Terry and Melba's first highly publicised collaboration was at what Terry anticipated in letters to Carew and Edith as Melba's 'big performance'. This took place on the 10th of September, at the 'Auditorium' in Melbourne and raised £1300–1500 for the Australian Red Cross in support of the Expeditionary force that was on the eve of its departure from Australia.[144] 'Melba's concert' reported widely in newspapers was of a more culturally refined tenor than the previous 'Patriotic Matinees.' It included performance of favourite opera arias and choral and orchestral pieces. Reporters provide lavish descriptions of the gowns worn by Melba and Terry. *The Herald* (Melbourne) quotes Melba calling it 'The greatest night of my career',[145] and indeed it was the beginning of Melba's new profile of philanthropic service for which she was made Dame Commander of the Order of the British Empire in 1918 and for which she is commemorated on the Australian hundred-dollar note.

Melba was the undisputed star of the show; Terry recited Rudyard Kipling's 'Big Steamers' – a sentimental celebration of England's dependence on goods transport from its furthest reaches by steam ships. In the performance of the poem, Terry is said to have shed tears and received generous accolades. It takes a little imagination for us to understand why anyone would find this poem so affecting, but if we consider the associations steamers would have had for Terry, the mystery unravels. In Sydney and Melbourne (which the poem mentions explicitly), steam ships dominated the coastal waterways – the pervasive sight, sound, and smell of them representing adventure and connection to other parts of the world and for Terry, the only way home. Her tears may well have been linked to her own grief of separation. For her audiences, no doubt, the sight of a statuesque, patrician British actress shedding her tears in their midst – as they shed their own in farewell to husbands, brothers, and sons bound for war zones in Europe – would have ratified the call to arms and made the world feel comfortingly smaller. It is not hard to imagine that Terry stood for Britannia herself in this ephemeral moment of performance.

Following Melba's 'big concert', Terry retreated once more with her friend to Coombe Cottage, and in this alternating rhythm of collaborative endeavour and rural retreat, she seems to have struck on a salutary formula. On the 18th of September, she writes to her daughter:

> This is an ideal spot, & Melba makes it an ideal <u>HOME</u> – she is so strong in body & character – quite a splendid <a magnific> woman = she is thinking out kindnesses every hour of the day – I just love her now = Oh, the garden here! – I've longed for you and Chris to be in it & I've ordered Roses for your Garden to be sent in the proper time ~~from~~ <by> this Gardener who takes <all>

---

[144] 'Music', *Punch* (Melbourne: 1900–1918; 1925), 17 September 1914, p. 9.
[145] 'Melba Gives Concert', *The Herald* (Melbourne: 1861–1954), 11 September 1914, p. 10.

> prizes year after year for them = I'm having some of the hedges photographed
> by young George Armstrong – <u>myrtle</u> hedges – they are in blossom now –
> great humps of berries …[146]

In the same month Terry evidently sends a photograph of Coombe Cottage with the message that 'No words can tell of the beauty of the various Gum Trees.'[147] Terry's energetic delight and investment in her surroundings is palpable on this communication which strains to share the pleasure she is experiencing in her new home away from home.

However, it was not all leisure on this extended visit to Coombe Cottage following Melba's concert in Melbourne. After less than a week the two embarked on a programme of local, smaller concerts:

> Melba is everlastingly promising to come & sing to <them> at this that & the
> other little village round about 50 miles of her home – & I went with her to
> some of the affairs – for she always keeps her promise I'm told – So I call
> myself "<u>touring with Mme Melba</u>" – !! I send you 2 cuttings – 15 & 17 Sep –
> I think you shd send them to some Paper

Terry and Melba performed together with others at the village of Lilydale close to Melba's home on the 14th of September and then only two days later at Warburton. Funds were raised for the local church and Mechanics Institute. Melba is quoted expressing great pride in the concerts that took place in and around her hometown – a refutation of the criticism that she cared 'not a fig for Australia and Australians'. She even organised a special train to take her and Terry from Lilydale to Warburton, collecting audience members along the way. *The Australasian* conveys the festival atmosphere:

> It was a merry party that left Lilydale by special train a few minutes after 6
> o'clock. Every station furnished its addition to the audience, and by the time
> the train pulled into Warburton station it was well filled. And at every station
> a group of eager people came pressing round the windows to catch a glimpse
> of the great singer. At Warburton itself a large crowd led by the reception
> committee, met Madame Melba at the station. The little main street was gay
> with festoons of Chinese lanterns and inside the Mechanics Institute, where
> the concert was held, the hall was prettily decorated with flowers and flags.
> When Madame Melba first came on to the platform she was met with
> a marvellous reception. The small building held a little over 300 but the
> audience made enough noise for a crowd four times its size. Miss Ellen Terry
> shared the triumph of her twin star. The audience enthusiastically encored
> her, and would have had yet more.[148]

---

[146] Terry and Cockin, *The Collected Letters*, V6. (1753. To Edith Craig, 18 September [1914]), p. 29.

[147] Ibid. (1754. To Edith Craig, September [1914]), p. 32.

[148] 'Musical notes', *Journal* (Adelaide: 1912–1923) 19 September 1914, p. 4.

A lovely touch in this account of small-town Australia's nights of glamour is remarked upon in many papers: 'In order to allow mothers, with large families at home and no one to "mind the baby," to attend, a temporary creche was established next door to the hall.'[149] This arrangement reflects that, despite the exceptionalism of their own privileged status, the two women created a climate that recognised and mitigated the constraints faced by other women caring for young children. The feminist initiative of free child-minding was such an unusual highlight that Melbourne's *Argus* headlines its report: 'Melba at Warburton: the creche and the concert.'[150] This generous, holiday atmosphere, the unalloyed delight of audiences, and creative collaboration for a cause seem to have galvanised Terry, by involving her in something greater than her own tour – making her a 'twin star' in a 'shared triumph'.

Melba's hospitality at home can only have added to the pleasure and stimulus of their shared appearances. Certainly, Terry hints at a newfound sense of belonging in her underlining and capitalisation when she claims that, 'This is an ideal spot, & Melba makes it an ideal <u>HOME</u>' (cited in footnote 146). Even their private connection was a source of public delight, especially in journalism produced by or intended for women. Papers as far away as *The Telegraph* (Brisbane) announced that 'Miss Ellen Terry is the guest of Madame Melba at Coombe Farm, Lilydale, Victoria'.[151] Melbourne's *Punch* seems to have an inside source for the goings on at Melba's property:

> It was a jolly house party at 'Coombe Cottage' last week and Madame Melba was perfectly in her element as hostess – there is no role that suits her better. The music, whiling away the evenings in the quaint drawing room up in the cottage in the hills, would have delighted and been sought after by many a crowned head of Europe. Melba creates around her an atmosphere – always artistic – of almost irresponsible gaiety and bonhomie. Last week's house party – who nearly all took part in the Warburton and Lilydale concerts – 'fitted' and amalgamated to perfection. It included Ellen Terry (as fellow star) [a list of other guests follows]. On Tuesday evening (last week) a special little party was given at 'Coombe Cottage,' when all the artist guests contributed items. Ellen Terry surpassed herself in some Juliet scenes [...] and Melba herself sang a quite new song specially written for her by Liza Lehmann just before her departure from England. [...] All this went on with no vestige of footlights, no flowers, and no guinea seats available.[152]

This evokes a backdrop against which we can imagine Terry hearing Melba 'sing The Blackbird' just for her (see Figure 6). In this way, Melba drew Terry

---

[149] 'Music', *Punch* (Melbourne: 1900–1918; 1925), 17 September 1914, p. 9.

[150] 'Melba at Warburton', *The Argus* (Melbourne: 1848–1957), 17 September 1914, p. 6.

[151] 'Ladies' Page', *The Telegraph* (Brisbane: 1872–1947*)*, 10 October 1914, p. 14.

[152] 'The Ladies Letter', *Punch* (Melbourne: 1900–1918; 1925*)*, 24 September 1914, p. 40.

Figure 6 'Boudoir at Coombe', Coombe Cottage, Coldstream, near Lilydale, Victoria, home of Dame Nellie Melba; Edwin G. Adamson (photographer); PIC BOX P1014 #P1014/1-4, National Library of Australia; https://nla.gov.au/nla .obj-142924197/view (out of copyright).

into a warm and welcoming community of artists embedded in a small village atmosphere which was like her own home in Kent.

One can only imagine the strange mix of solace and disappointment the women experienced during this enforced pause at the zenith of their careers. Nevertheless, Terry's admiration of Melba's garden and Australian native flora is rapturous. In a letter to G B Shaw written later that year she exclaims that 'Australia is a Garden'.[153] That Australia left an indelible mark upon Terry's imagination is attested in a casual reference she makes to 'that wonderful Australia' in a letter written to Dorothy Allunsen when she was back at Smallhythe the following year.[154]

A ten-minute film of Melba at her property in 1927 provides some further tantalising glimpses into how Terry and Melba may have spent their time

---

[153] Terry and Cockin, *The Collected Letters*, V6. (1771. 'To George Bernard Shaw, [1914]), p. 59.
[154] Terry and Cockin, *The Collected Letters*, V6. (1796. To Dorothy Allunsen, 10 July [1915]), p. 84.

together.[155] All of the footage is shot outdoors. It includes sequences of Melba speaking with her adult son, George, and his wife, Evie, and her nine-year-old granddaughter, Pamela. Animals feature prominently – a black spaniel, a pony, and a pet cockatoo in a cage, whom Melba jokingly berates with pointed finger. Melba and the other women pluck flowers from bushes and hold them up in various arrangements or pretend to conduct with them. In one sequence Melba collects white daises which off-set her own pale cloak, hat, and shoes. At sixty-six years of age – the same age Terry was in 1914 – Melba moves in playful fashion, stopping to pose in a self-conscious way for the camera before making a dramatic exit that sends her cape whirling.

There is a poignant sense of awkwardness in the way Melba and Terry appear in the relatively new medium of film. After her Jubilee and return to England, Terry featured in some films but the footage, flickering and grainy, reveals a hesitant, disorientated old woman. I have attempted to tell a new story of friendship that reveals Terry's vitality, energy, resourcefulness, sense of fun, and beauty, but it is a story that begins where others have seen only a protracted ending taking place, at the end of the earth.

It must have been an emotional farewell at the end of October when Terry boarded the *Makura* for Auckland – the first of many legs on a long journey home to England (see Figure 7). In a letter to Edith as she leaves Sydney Terry says, 'I've made a good many pleasant acquaintances & a few good friends in New Z. & Australia [...] then Melba who is a jolly good friend & who has put heaps of thoughtful comforts on board this Makura for me.'[156] Both women were ageing stars – Melba approaching her zenith and Terry having passed hers – heading into a long, dark night with the world at war. In a letter to James Carew on the 5th of November, Terry describes her eerie journey across the Pacific: '... we are travelling with only about 33 passengers (all told) on this big ship (and we put all the lights out at night, – & the drifting on mysteriously in the darkness is rather creepy & wonderful.'[157]

Terry's capacity to find wonder in the expanse of blackness, even, ironically as her own eyesight was failing, is a testament to her enduringly intrepid spirit. The narrative arc imposed by Christopher St John, followed by more recent scholarship has hitherto emphasised the hardship of Terry's tour to Australia and New Zealand. Without question it was beset with illness, worry, and longing for home; but the traveller's experience is not the same as the account impro-vised by those whom she leaves behind. In her letters home and in her comments to the local press, Terry's anxiety and sadness are balanced with vital curiosity

---

[155] 'Dame Nellie Melba at Coombe Cottage', November 1927.
[156] Terry and Cockin, *The Collected Letters*, V6. (1758. To Edith Craig, 30 October [1914]), pp. 7, 36.
[157] Ibid. (1759. To James Carew, 5 November [1914]), p. 38.

Figure 7 'S. S. Makura at dock', before 1949, Walter E. Frost (photographer), black and white nitrate negative, 6 × 11 cm; City of Vancouver Archives; https://searcharchives.vancouver.ca/s-s-makura-at-dock (public domain).

and enjoyment. In her unsolicited expressions of delight, we get a sense of her distinctive openness to new people and places. She registers how these permitted her to re-make herself, and she knowingly used her newfound connection with them to mitigate prejudicial responses to her age and gender.

Afterword

In her set of lectures published as *A Room of One's Own* in 1928 – the year of Ellen Terry's death and the year in which all women above the age of twenty were granted suffrage in Britain – Virginia Woolf asserts that women, like men, have other interests than domesticity. She points out that stories have rarely been told of the positive relationship formed between women in the course of pursuing their professions. In a hypothetical story written by 'Mary Carmichael', she describes reading that 'Chloe liked Olivia' and that 'they shared a laboratory'. Woolf celebrates 'a moment in which something of great importance has happened' – a narrative of a friendship between two women that is 'more varied and more lasting because it is less personal'.[158]

Paying careful attention to the extant evidence we have of the friendship that formed between Nellie Melba and Ellen Terry during Terry's arguably ill-timed and ill-fated visit to Australia reveals that one such friendship had already blossomed in a sphere (and hemisphere) that evaded Woolf's notice. The touring actress, through her mobility and relationships was already establishing

---

[158] Woolf, *A Room of One's Own*, pp. 81–83.

a new narrative stride: discovering collegial mutuality and even making the world more habitable and navigable through a shared receptivity to its natural wonders. There is a great deal of work still to be done in understanding touring actresses as vectors of change in movements of political modernity. I have suggested that the spatial turn, used to historicise the feminist geography of the touring actress, opens a story that might begin, rather than end, like this: Nellie liked Ellen, and they shared a stage.

This Element has advocated that a hidden chapter in Ellen Terry's own life be opened, investigated, and enjoyed. Circumstances that have conspired to keep it closed until now include an approach to theatre history that dismisses New Zealand and Australia as of marginal interest because they are marginal to a trans-Atlantic locus of theatre history. In the case of Ellen Terry, this dismissal has been compounded by an entrenched discourse of gendered ageism in the performing arts. The implicit surmise of twentieth-century scholars was that wanting to go so far so late in life could only indicate that Terry was 'not all there'. Sadly, in this assumption, even feminist scholars have unwittingly colluded with some of Terry's most misogynistic detractors. A more benign version of the story has origins in Christopher St John's account of Terry as a self-sacrificing matriarch, prepared to undertake the venture to support her family. While there may be grains of truth in each of these explanations for the tour, they overlook factors that this Element brings to light.

The first is that for Terry, raised in the nineteenth century, in a family of itinerant players, touring was a natural way of life. Following in the steps of many other international stars, Terry may have seen the gold-rush locations of Australia and New Zealand as obvious rather than odd destinations. The oft-cited tensions in her domestic context along with her own intrepid but informed curiosity about new places may well have further galvanised her determination to go. But leaving speculation aside, this Element has sought to pay close attention to the documented facts of her own experience and those of her audiences. The scholarly edited publication of Terry's collected letters by Katharine Cockin and the affordances of digitised newspapers, papers, and photographs have made it possible to join the dots across the globe and present a version of Terry's tour that is closer to how Terry experienced it.

This has shed new light on the ambition, creative innovation and resilience she demonstrated, along with the benefits the tour conferred upon her. Her repertoire – the Shakespeare's women 'discourses' – facilitated a new kind of artistic control and a new kind of relationship with new audiences. They capitalised in a canny way on Terry's international prestige as a supreme player of Shakespeare, but they also gave her scope to critique the male-dominated London theatre context in which she had achieved it. In Australia and New

Zealand the Shakespeare discourses were a newly situated act of feminist revision; even so, they were not purely backward looking. Terry's prominence as a 'pioneer player' in the British drama for women's suffrage made her a visionary for the enfranchised women of the Commonwealth countries, allowing them to see themselves, in turn, as the vanguard of a heroic international movement. Finally, Terry's evolving relationship with Nellie Melba, sharpened by a shared love of Australia's distinctive natural environment, is a microcosm of professional friendship – an important but infrequently noted dynamic of the international women's movement in the early decades of the twentieth century.

Bibliography

Auerbach, Nina, *Ellen Terry, Player in Her Time*, 1st ed. (New York: W.W. Norton, 1987).

Bachmann-Medick, Doris. *Cultural Turns: New Orientations in the Study of Culture* (Berlin: De Gruyter, 2016).

Balme, Christopher, *The Globalization of Theatre 1870–1930: The Theatrical Networks of Maurice E. Bandmann* (Cambridge: Cambridge University Press, 2019).

Beebe, Kathryne, and Angela Davis, (eds.), *Space, Place and Gendered Identities: Feminist History and the Spatial Turn* (London: Routledge, Taylor & Francis Group, 2015).

Booth, Michael R., 'Ellen Terry', in John Stokes, Michael R. Booth, and Susan Bassnett, *Bernhardt, Terry, Duse: The Actress in Her Time* (Cambridge: Cambridge University Press, 1988), pp. 65–117.

Bratton, Jacky, 'Frances Anne Kemble', in Gail Marshall (ed.) *Jameson, Cowden Clarke, Kemble, Cushman: Great Shakespeareans* (Bloomsbury: London, 2014), vol. VII, pp. 120–32.

Bratton, Jacky, and Gilli Bush-Bailey, 'Bodies of Evidence: The Unremarkable History of Emma Stanley (1816–1881)', in Gilli Bush-Bailey and Kate Flaherty (eds.) *Touring Performance and Global Exchange 1850–1960: Making Tracks* (Oxford: Taylor & Francis Group, 2021), pp. 48–64.

Caine, Barbara, 'Australian Feminism and the British Militant Suffragettes', in *Papers on Parliament*, 41 (June 2004). www.aph.gov.au/About_Parliament/Senate/Powers_practice_n_procedures/~/~/link.aspx?_id=3C44655A04494661A14BF77C89E93438&_z=z.

Cannon, Michael, 'Norton, John (1858–1916)', first published in Geoffrey Serle (General Editor) *Australian Dictionary of Biography* (Australian National University: National Centre of Biography, 1988), vol XI, 51; online in 2006. https://adb.anu.edu.au/biography/norton-john-7863/text13663 published first in hardcopy 1988.

Cockin, Katharine, *Women and Theatre in the Age of Suffrage: The Pioneer Players, 1911–1925* (Hampshire: Palgrave, 2001).

Cockin, Katharine, 'Ellen Terry, the Ghost-Writer and the Laughing Statue; the Victorian Actress, Letters and Life-Writing', *Journal of European Studies*, 32 (2002), pp. 151–63.

Cockin, Katharine, 'Slinging the Ink about: Ellen Terry and Women's Suffrage Agitation', in Caroline Bland and Marie Cross (eds.) *Gender Politics in the Age of Letter-Writing, 1750–2000* (Aldershot: Ashgate, 2004), pp. 201–12.

'Dame Nellie Melba at Coombe Cottage', November 1927, National Film and Sound Archive (Australia) NFSA ID: 1064169 www.nfsa.gov.au/collection/curated/asset/99886-dame-nellie-melba-coombe-cottage-november-1927-full-clip.

Davidson, Jim, 'Melba, Dame Nellie (1861–1931)', first published in Bede Nairn and Geoffrey Serle (General Editors) *Australian Dictionary of Biography* (Australian National University: National Centre of Biography, 1986), vol X, 522; online in 2006. https://adb.anu.edu.au/biography/melba-dame-nellie-7551/text13175 published first in hardcopy 1986.

Deacon, Deacon, Penny Russell, and Angela Woollacott, 'Introduction', in Desley Deacon, Penny Russell, and Angela Woollacott (eds.) *Transnational Lives: Biographies of Global Modernity, 1700–present* (Basingstoke: Palgrave Macmillan, 2010), pp. 1–11.

Faucit, Helena (Lady Martin), *On Some of Shakespeare's Female Characters*, (London: William Blackwood and Sons, 1885).

Flaherty, Kate and Edel Lamb, 'The 1863 Melbourne Shakespeare War: Barry Sullivan, Charles and Ellen Kean, and the Play of Cultural Usurpation on the Australian Stage', *Australian Studies*, 4 (2012), pp. 1–17.

Holton, Sandra Stanley, 'Women's Social and Political Union (act. 1903–1914)', in *Oxford Dictionary of National Biography*. 24 May 2008. www.oxforddnb.com/view/10.1093/ref:odnb/9780198614128.001.0001/odnb-9780198614128-e-95579.

Jermyn, Deborah, '"Get a Life, Ladies. Your Old One Is Not Coming Back": Ageing, Ageism and the Lifespan of Female Celebrity', *Celebrity Studies*, 3:1 (2012), pp. 1–12. https://doi.org/10.1080/19392397.2012.644708.

Kazmier, Lisa, 'Her Final Performance: British Culture, Mourning and the Memorialization of Ellen Terry', *Mortality*, 6:2 (2001), pp. 167–90.

Kelly, Katherine E., 'The after Voice of Ellen Terry', in Katharine Cockin (ed.), *Ellen Terry: Spheres of Influence* (London: Pickering and Chatto, 2011), pp. 65–76.

Leonhardt, Nic, *Theatre across Oceans: Mediators of Transatlantic Exchange, 1890–1925*, 1st ed. (Cham: Springer International; Imprint: Palgrave Macmillan, 2021) https://doi.org/10.1007/978-3-030-76355-8.

Liddy, Susan, (ed.), *Women, Ageing and the Screen Industries: Falling off a Cliff?* (Cham: Palgrave Macmillan, 2023).

Manvell, Roger, *Ellen Terry* (London: Heinemann, 1968).

Marshall, Gail, *Actresses on the Victorian Stage: Feminine Performance and the Galatea Myth* (Cambridge: Cambridge University Press, 1998).

Marshall, Gail, 'Ellen Terry: Shakespearean Actress and Critic', *European Journal of Women's Studies*, 11:3 (2004), pp. 355–64.

Massey, Doreen B., *Space, Place, and Gender* (Minneapolis: University of Minnesota Press, 1994).

Merrill, Lisa, 'Charlotte Cushman', in Gail Marshall (ed.), *Jameson, Cowden Clarke, Kemble, Cushman: Great Shakespeareans* (Bloomsbury: London, 2014), vol. VII, pp. 169–79.

Rose, Gillian, *Feminism and Geography: The Limits of Geographical Knowledge*, (Minneapolis: University of Minnesota Press, 1993).

Scott, Myra, *How Australia Led the Way: Dora Meeson Coates and British Suffrage, Commonwealth Office of the Status of Women* (Australia: Australian Government: Department of Prime Minister and Cabinet, 2003) www.aph.gov.au/-/media/06_Visit_Parliament/Parl_House_Art_Collection/Women_and_suffrage/Scott_Meeson_suffrage_banner.pdf?la=en&hash=F379DF947F3454ED57EE0C0531807A898A157FD9.

Terry, Ellen, Bernard Shaw, and Christopher St John, *Ellen Terry and Bernard Shaw* (London: Constable, 1931).

Terry, Ellen, *Four Lectures on Shakespeare*, Christopher St John (ed.) (London: M. Hopkinson, 1932).

Terry, Ellen, Edith Craig, and Christopher St John, *Ellen Terry's Memoirs: With Preface, Notes and Additional Biographical Chapters* (London: Gollancz, 1933).

Terry, Ellen, and Katharine Cockin, *The Collected Letters of Ellen Terry. Vol. 6 1914–1928*, (London: Pickering & Chatto, 2015).

Thiong'o, Ngũgĩ wa, *Globaletics: Theory and the Politics of Knowing* (New York: Columbia University Press, 2012).

Van Der Poorten, Helen M., 'Jennings, Elizabeth Esther Helen (1864–1920)', first published in Douglas Pike (General Editor) *Australian Dictionary of Biography* (National Centre of Biography, Australian National University, 1972), vol IV, 594; online in 2006. https://adb.anu.edu.au/biography/jennings-elizabeth-esther-helen-3855/text6129, published first in hardcopy 1972, accessed online 19 November 2024.

West, Shearer, 'Siddons, Celebrity and Regality: Portraiture and the Body of the Ageing Actress', in Mary Luckhurst and Jane Moody (eds.) *Theatre and Celebrity in Britain, 1660–2000* (London: Palgrave Macmillan, 2005), pp. 191–213. https://doi.org/10.1057/9780230523845_11.

Wiet, Victoria, 'The Actress in Nature: Environments of Artistic Development in Victorian Fiction and Memoir', *Nineteenth Century Theatre and Film*, 45:2 (2018), pp. 232–53.

Woodward, Kathleen, *Figuring Age: Women, Bodies, Generations* (Bloomington: Indiana University Press, 1999).

Woolf, Virginia, *A Room of One's Own* (1928) (London: Penguin, 1945).

Newspaper Articles

'Amusements', *Harrisburg Telegraph*, 18 February 1915, p. 4. https://chroni clingamerica.loc.gov/lccn/sn85038411/1915-01-26/ed-1/seq-9/.

'Amusements: Ellen Terry', *The Star-independent* (Harrisburg), 21 January 1914. https://chroniclingamerica.loc.gov/lccn/sn86081330/1915-01-21/ed-1/seq-8/.

'Arrival of Miss Ellen Terry', *The Queenslander*, Saturday 30 May 1914, p. 6. https://trove.nla.gov.au/newspaper/article/25507130.

'A Charming Personality', *North Otago Times*, 13 July 1914, p. 6. https:// paperspast.natlib.govt.nz/newspapers/NOT19140713.2.55.

'Corner Chronicles', *Truth* (Sydney: 1894–1954), 17 May 1896, p. 2. http://nla .gov.au/nla.news-article169754996.

'The Critic', *Truth* (Sydney: 1894–1954), 3 November 1895, p. 1. http://nla.gov .au/nla.news-article167954382.

'Dramatic Notes', *Leader* (Melbourne: 1862–1918, 1935), 24 October 1914, p. 37. http://nla.gov.au/nla.news-article92032737.

'Ellen Terry: Arrival in Auckland', *Auckland Star* (New Zealand), 1 June 1914, p. 7.

'Ellen Terry: Arrival in Australia', *Northern Advocate*, 1 May 1914, p. 5. https://paperspast.natlib.govt.nz/newspapers/NA19140501.2.23.

'Ellen Terry', *Daily Standard* (Brisbane: 1912–1936), 21 May 1914, p. 6. http:// nla.gov.au/nla.news-article178881969.

'Ellen Terry', *Darling Downs Gazette* (Queensland) 21 May 1914, p. 6. http:// nla.gov.au/nla.news-article186865057.

'Ellen Terry', *Evening Post* (Wellington), 19 June 1914, p. 2. https://paperspast .natlib.govt.nz/newspapers/EP19140619.2.10.

'Ellen Terry in Town', *The Telegraph* (Brisbane: 1872–1947), 21 May 1914, p. 8. http://nla.gov.au/nla.news-article176218676.

'Ellen Terry Sails for Home', *New York Tribune*, 2 May 1915, p. 3. https:// chroniclingamerica.loc.gov/lccn/sn83030214/1915-05-02/ed-1/seq-3/.

'Ellen Terry Will Hear Senator Clapp', *Harrisburg Telegraph*, 26 January 1915, p. 4. https://chroniclingamerica.loc.gov/lccn/sn85038411/1915-01-26/ed-1/seq-4/.

'For Women Folk by "Chryssa"', *Star* (Christchurch), 13 April 1914, p. 7. https://paperspast.natlib.govt.nz/newspapers/TS19140413.2.78.

The Freewoman I.1 (23 November 1911) quoted in Katharine Cockin, *Women and Theatre in the Age of Suffrage: The Pioneer Players, 1911–1925* (Hampshire: Palgrave, 2001), p. 49.

'A Geebung Goddess', *Truth* (Sydney: 1894–1954) 16 June 1901, p. 3. http://nla.gov.au/nla.news-article168004435.

'Gossip for Women', *The Week* (Brisbane: 1876–1934), 29 May 1914, p. 8. http://nla.gov.au/nla.news-article185009600.

'His Last Cup', *Worker* (Brisbane: 1890–1955), 18 June 1914, p. 12. http://nla.gov.au/nla.news-article70887830.

'Holding on Too Long', *Northern Daily Advocate* (New Zealand), 2 April 1927, p. 4. https://paperspast.natlib.govt.nz/newspapers/NA19270402.2.13.

'Ladies Letter', *Table Talk* (Melbourne: 1885–1939), 17 September 1914, p. 28. http://nla.gov.au/nla.news-article146328794.

'The Ladies Letter', *Punch* (Melbourne: 1900–1918; 1925), 24 September 1914, p. 40. http://nla.gov.au/nla.news-article121086309.

'Ladies' Page', *The Telegraph* (Brisbane: 1872–1947), 10 October 1914, p. 14. http://nla.gov.au/nla.news-article177935735.

'Lights-O'-Lunnon', Special for *Truth* by Mary Brown (Melbourne) 30 May 1914. https://trove.nla.gov.au/newspaper/title/699 and http://adb.anu.edu.au/biography/norton-john-7863.

'Madame Melba's Aid', *The Australasian* (Melbourne: 1864–1946), 19 September 1914, p. 28. http://nla.gov.au/nla.news-article143287474.

'Melba at Warburton', *The Argus* (Melbourne: 1848–1957), 17 September 1914, p. 6 http://nla.gov.au/nla.news-article10807001.

'Melba Gives Concert', *The Herald* (Melbourne: 1861–1954), 11 September 1914, p. 10. http://nla.gov.au/nla.news-article242303529.

'Melbourne Social Notes', *Bendigo Advertiser* (Bendigo, Victoria: 1855–1918), 17 September 1914, p. 4. http://nla.gov.au/nla.news-article90530122.

'Miss Ellen Terry', *Table Talk* (Melbourne: 1885–1939), 14 May 1914, p. 10. http://nla.gov.au/nla.news-article14632087.

'Miss Ellen Terry', *The Argus* (Melbourne: 1848–1957), 23 January 1915, p. 6. http://nla.gov.au/nla.news-article1491751.

'Miss Ellen Terry's Departure', *The Sydney Morning Herald* (Sydney: 1842–1954), 30 October 1914, p. 5.

'Mr. Blascheck's Recital', *The Argus* (Melbourne: 1848–1957), 27 October 1914, p. 10. http://nla.gov.au/nla.news-article10813936.

'Music', *Punch* (Melbourne: 1900–1918; 1925), 17 September 1914, p. 9. http://nla.gov.au/nla.news-article121086101.

'Musical notes', *Journal* (Adelaide: 1912–1923) 19 September 1914, p. 4. https://nla.gov.au/nla.news-article210030205.

'News of the Day', *Evening News* (Sydney: 1869–1931), Friday 27 March 1874, p. 2. https://trove.nla.gov.au/newspaper/article/107144163.

'Not a Militant', *The Sun* (Sydney: 1910–1954), 13 May 1914, p. 9. http://nla .gov.au/nla.news-article224648286.

'Opinion of an Actress', *The Bennington Evening Banner* (Vermont) 13 January 1915, image 2. https://chroniclingamerica.loc.gov/lccn/sn95066012/1915-01-13/ed-1/seq-2/.

'The Patriotic Matinees', *Punch* (Melbourne: 1900–1918; 1925), 27 August 1914, p. 44. http://nla.gov.au/nla.news-article121085557.

'Personal', *The Australasian* (Melbourne: 1864–1946), 15 August 1914, p. 29. http://nla.gov.au/nla.news-article143285578.

Poverty Bay Herald (NZ), 10 June 1914, p. 2. https://paperspast.natlib.govt.nz/newspapers/PBH19140610.2.9.

'The Suffragettes', *Weekly Times* (Melbourne: 1869–1954), 13 June 1914, p. 1 http://nla.gov.au/nla.news-article121131257.

'Sydney Snapshots', *Truth* (Brisbane: 1900–1954), 9 August 1914, p. 12. http://nla.gov.au/nla.news-article202658939.

'Two Actresses', *The Sydney Morning Herald* (Sydney: 1842–1954), 25 July 1914, p. 8. http://nla.gov.au/nla.news-article15525400.

'When I Was a Girl', *The Journal* (Adelaide: 1912–1923), 2 May 1914, p. 6. http://nla.gov.au/nla.news-article204667097.

'Woman's World', *The Brisbane Courier* (Brisbane: 1864–1933), 21 May 1914, p. 9. http://nla.gov.au/nla.news-article19964239.

Acknowledgements

I am grateful to Professor Penny Gay and Professor Joanne Tompkins for careful reading and thoughtful feedback in the process of writing this book. I have Justin to thank for patient proof-reading and Emily Wotherspoon for wonderful research assistance. I thank Professor Gilli Bush-Bailey and Professor Jacky Bratton for collaborating with me on the symposium on touring theatre at which this research first saw light – bright, Australian light. Through their support of that symposium, Professor Will Christie and the Humanities Research Centre at ANU, along with Professor Rae Frances and the College of Arts and Social Sciences at ANU were also key players. Finally, I am grateful to Elaine Aston for taking on this Element with such enthusiasm and to the team at Cambridge University Press for helping it come into being.

For Gilli, and to friendship in defiance of distance.

* 9 7 8 1 0 0 9 5 5 9 3 3 1 *